PETER SEABROOK'S
COMPLETE VEGETABLE GARDENER

Cassell & Company Limited
35 Red Lion Square, London, WC1R 4SG,
and at Sydney, Auckland, Toronto, Johannesburg,
an affiliate of Macmillan Publishing Co., Inc.,
New York

Designed and produced for Cassell & Company by
Intercontinental Book Productions
Berkshire House, Queen Street, Maidenhead, Berks.
Copyright © 1976 by Intercontinental Book Productions

First published 1976
ISBN 0 304 29738 0
Printed in Yugoslavia

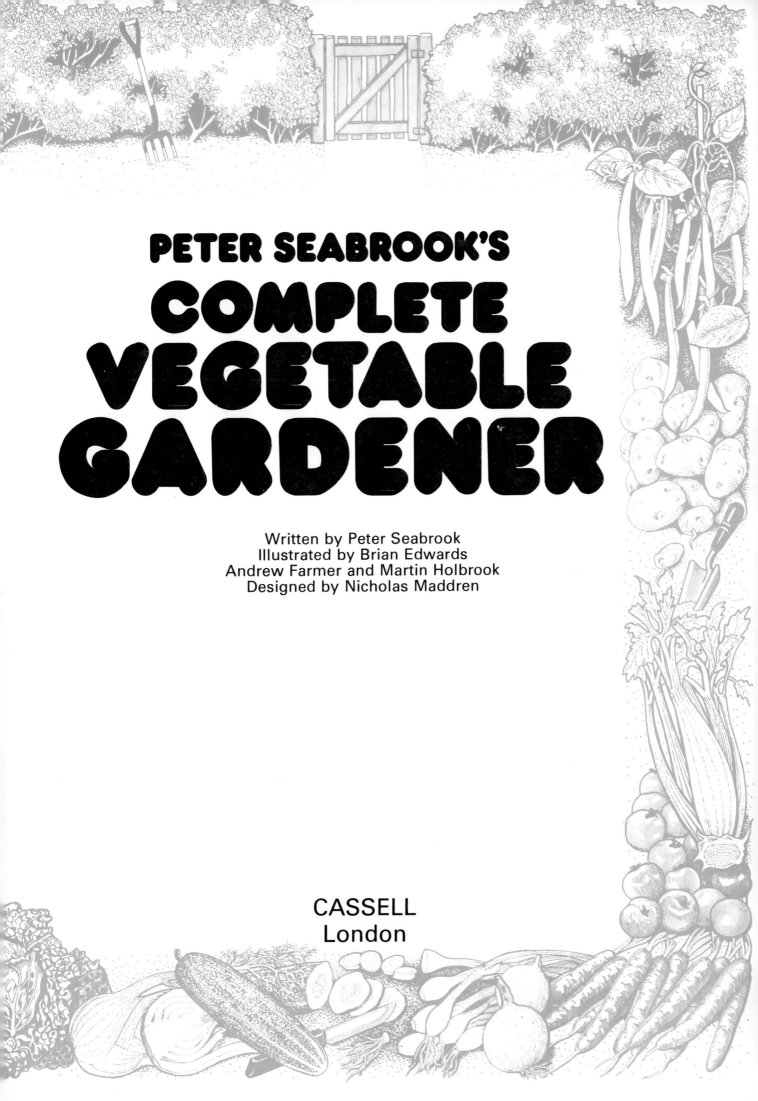

PETER SEABROOK'S COMPLETE VEGETABLE GARDENER

Written by Peter Seabrook
Illustrated by Brian Edwards
Andrew Farmer and Martin Holbrook
Designed by Nicholas Maddren

CASSELL
London

Contents

Introduction

Growing vegetables in the garden used to be an accepted part of life – something that everyone did and no one thought a great deal about. In the mid-decades of this century, this practice became somewhat superseded by the cultivation of ornamental, rather than edible plants, but ever-rising food prices and current economic problems have brought it very much back into the limelight. Now, people are anxious to know how to make the most of the land available to them as well as how best to cultivate different types of vegetables for maximum yield and greatest variety.

It is against this background that the 'Dig This' television series was introduced to millions of viewers. In this programme, we proved that even with a tiny plot of land at our disposal – a mere 10 ft × 12 ft (3 m × 4 m) – a variety of fresh vegetables can be produced *each week of the year*. A minimum of time and money – precious commodities in today's world – is required to achieve this steady flow of produce. This information is now available to everyone within the pages of this book, and although emphasis is placed on the small plot, those with more – or even less – land will find the book just as useful. This is because full cultural instructions are given for each individual vegetable, with tips and hints on how to utilise patio, balcony, and windowsill areas.

The book is divided into several sections covering all the major aspects of vegetable growing, among them the siting of the vegetable plot in the garden, necessary tools and equipment, how to recognise and improve soil, raising seeds, the importance of crop rotation (particularly in the small plot), some hints on the use of cloches, frames and simple greenhouses, and how to recognise and control weeds, pests and diseases. The principle and workings of the 10 ft × 12 ft (3 m × 4 m) plot are explained with various plans to show how best to use the plot for your own requirements. Several charts show you at a glance the economics of growing vegetables, how long seed will last before losing its germination factor, exactly when to sow and harvest each vegetable so your land need never be unproductive, and how to store and keep them. It is worth spending time perusing these sections before studying the book's largest section, from page 40 onwards, in which the individual cultural requirements of each vegetable are described.

The practical and economic aspects of vegetable cultivation have been overriding concerns in the writing of this book, for there is undoubtedly great pleasure and satisfaction in producing succulent, fresh vegetables throughout the year at a fraction of the cost of their older, less flavoursome shop counterparts. In addition there are few people who do not find enjoyment in seeing things grow – and the physical exertion of gardening, even in the small doses we recommend, is both therapeutic and inexpensive.

The Vegetable Plot in your Garden

When professional landscapers talk about garden design, it should be remembered that they have a background of training and experience in the artistic use of plants and garden accessories on both a large and small scale. For most of us, however, gardening is a series of compromises. The average family will make a number of demands on the immediate area surrounding their house – at least on that which constitutes their 'territory'. It is necessary from the point of view of property value, as well as for aesthetic reasons to keep the garden tidy and attractive all the year round. Hedges and fences are needed to establish boundaries, as well as giving protection from wind and providing some degree of privacy.

Children and adults will have different requirements from a garden, but both needs can be considered at planning stage. Children will doubtless want some grassy area for playing and

Left: Many features have been fitted into this small suburban garden.
Right: Vegetables growing in the author's garden.
Below: Figure 1: Vegetable plot featured in the patio area. Figure 2: Vegetable plot in full view of the house.

Figure 1.

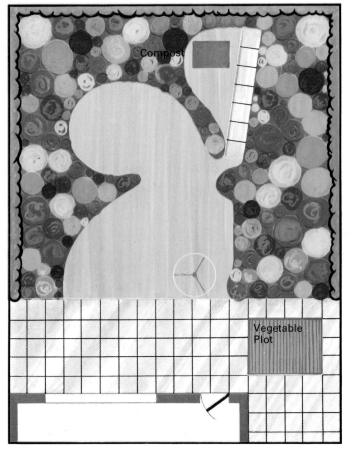

Figure 2.

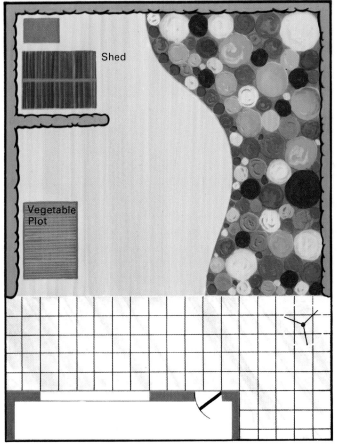

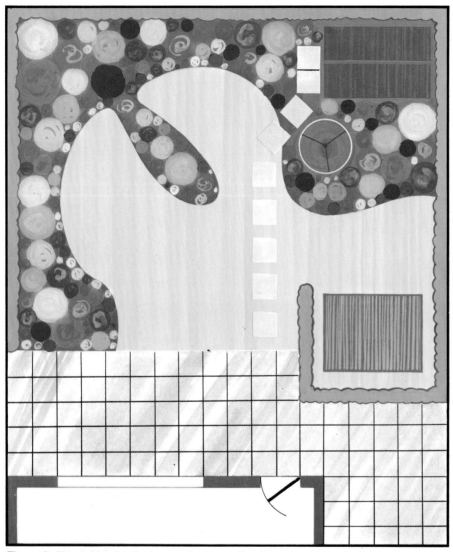

Figure 3: Vegetable plot is close to the house, but is screened by a hedge.

draw up a list of all the features and utilities you want to include and then cut each out to a scaled size. Mark out the total garden shape and size to the same scale on a large sheet of paper and then try a variety of combinations and arrangements to see how you can fit everything together in the most pleasing way.

Whether making a new start in a new garden or revamping an old one, first establish the boundaries, by planting hedges and erecting fences to give protection as soon as possible; next, cultivate the garden, making it level before sowing grass seed, laying paths and paving. After seeding, it is easy to cut out the beds, borders and vegetable plot area.

The Vegetable Plot

If you have a modern, virtually square, garden and wish to fit in a 10 ft × 12 ft (3 × 4 m) vegetable plot for example (see page 22), there are a number of ways of doing so (see figures 1, 2, 3 and 8). You could either site it so it is hidden away or so it is in full view from the house or patio area, and this will depend on how you feel about it individually. I find great pleasure in looking at a vegetable plot packed full of vigorously growing rows of plants in June, but the sight of overwintering greens, I find less appealing. On the other hand I love to see beautifully dug earth – all neat and level in a winter plot.

perhaps a swing and sandpit. Adults are likely to be happy with just a grassy area for summer sitting-out and relaxation! Then provision should also be made for a shed in which to keep tools and garden tables and chairs; for a compost area and a bonfire or incinerator site; perhaps an ornamental pool for fish and storage space for a boat or caravan as well as a path to give access to a clothes line. To most people, bringing all their requirements together within the strict confines of the area available to them, stretches an ability to 'design' a garden to the limit!

Great improvements can be made to an existing layout, however, with just a little careful planning. At a time of reorganisation, whether it be that you are faced with what is a completely new garden to you, or whether you merely feel it is time to make a few major changes to your existing garden, do allow yourself time to really *plan* the future arrangement. Ideally,

Figure 4: Some typical garden shapes.

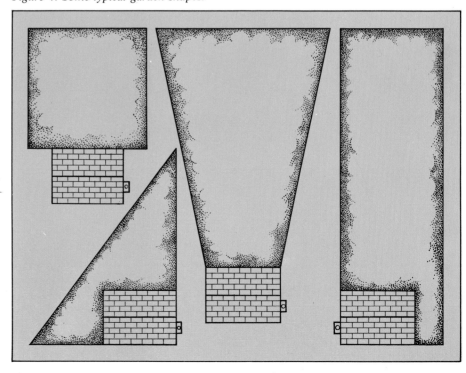

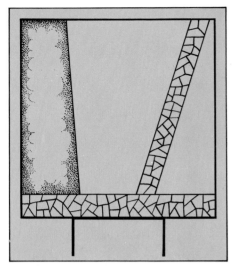

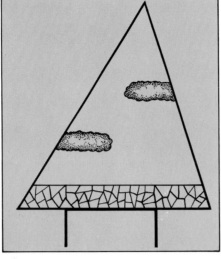

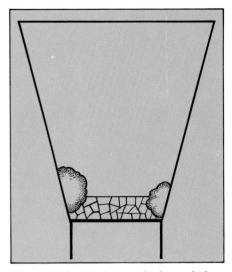

Figure 5: Paths and borders help to make a square garden look longer.

Figure 6: Cleverly placed hedges hide converging lines of a triangle.

Figure 7: Shrubs close to the house hide closely fenced boundaries.

Generally speaking there are three basic garden shapes; square, rectangular and triangular (see figure 4). Having the vegetable area in sight or out of view can be alternatives whichever basic shape you have. It is important, however, to watch and plan the angle of paths and screens in the extreme cases.

If a garden is completely square you can make it look longer by placing two paths or a path and border so that they slant away from one another to give diverging lines instead of converging lines (see figure 5). Similar treatment will help to broaden the appearance of a narrow garden.

The definite outer lines of triangular gardens can be softened by strategic planting of evergreen shrubs and screens. Where the house is at the base of the triangle, as it were, a screen jutting out from one side (see figure 6) will help hide the converging sides. If, on the other hand, the wide part of the garden triangle is at the bottom of the garden, planting bushy shrubs close to the house will help to hide the closely fenced boundaries (see figure 7).

Lawns and Paths
When you are planning to sow or lay turf for a lawn, aim to keep it in one area of garden only. It is not only then easier to mow, but gives the largest area for adults to sit and children to play and also helps prevent the garden from looking too fragmented. Paths are important, especially close by the vegetable plot for you will want to be able to get to the vegetables in wet weather without getting your feet muddy. If there is a path surrounding the plot, it is also easier to cultivate –

you can hoe and weed from either side with a minimum of trampling over wet soil.

The siting of clean, dry paths must also be included in your plans, so that clothes lines, compost heaps, etc., are all easily accessible.

Don't discard the possibility of growing vegetables to form temporary summer screens. Obvious and attractive examples are runner beans grown up poles, with their scarlet, white or combination-coloured flowers and the jerusalem artichoke.

Figure 8: Vegetable plot placed at the end of the garden. Both here and in Figure 3 a compost heap could be made close to the hedge.

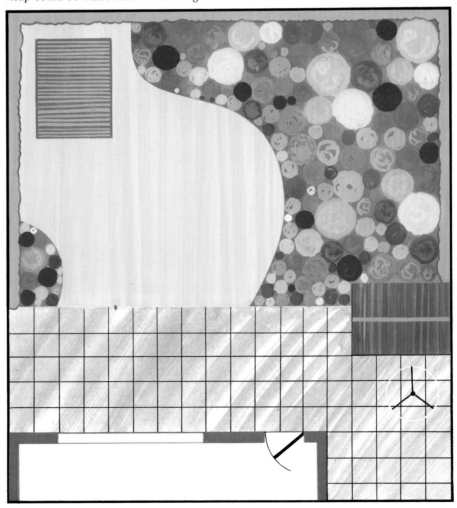

Essential Gardening Equipment

Lack of sophisticated gardening tools is no obstacle when it comes to vegetable growing – in fact your basic requirements are no more than a spade, a piece of wood and a length of string! The spade is fundamental to the whole operation and if you have a good spade, which you learn to handle adeptly, it will do very nearly every job that needs doing during vegetable growing.

Buy the Best

Although a spade is the bare minimum, I am in no way against owning a range of tools and certainly, for the new gardener, having the right tool for the job will make things easier. You must, however, always buy good tools – cheap inferior ones are invariably a bad buy. I can assure you, in buying tools, it is your economies you will regret, never your extravagancies.

Working through a list of tools in a rough and ready order of priority, as I have already made clear, the spade comes first. The range of different types is formidable – certainly as many as forty to fifty with quite fundamental differences. Nevertheless, this is an improvement on a few years ago when there were nearer two hundred different types! Choose the type of spade which suits you personally – as a traditionalist I prefer those with wooden handles, but admittedly the new polypropylene handles are much more resistant to wet and other climatic conditions. Heavy, wet soils are easier to dig using a very shiny stainless steel spade, as the wet soil slips off the blade, but bear in mind that stainless steel tools are more expensive than those made of ordinary steel. If an ordinary steel spade is wiped clean after use and perhaps rubbed over with an oily rag to retain the shine, it will be quite as easy and comfortable to use.

Comfort is Important

Note the word 'comfortable' for that is the important thing to bear in mind when choosing tools. Generally speaking, although the stainless steel types are more expensive, they are usually more comfortable to use and easier to keep in clean working order.

One point to watch when buying a spade is the finish on the 'tread' (i.e. the spot where you push the spade into the ground with your foot). Many modern designs have a straight edge at the tread, while others have a small flat piece of metal. Although wet soil may stick to this as you dig the soil, it does

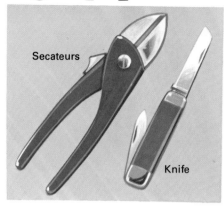

Figure 9.

protect your instep, but it may be that you will find a spade with a metal tread most useful when gardening on lighter soils.

Besides digging, you can use a spade rather like a hoe for weed control. Just chip the top surface area working backwards between rows to chop out weeds and leave a very neat finish. Use the corner of a spade to draw out seed drills against a line.

A garden line, comprising just two sticks with a piece of string tied

Figure 10.

between them, is useful to keep rows of vegetables straight at sowing and planting time.

Irrigation equipment

A watering can is a fairly essential piece of equipment; generally the thing to remember is that the longer the spout, the lower the angle of the spout to the ground when you are watering. This means you can give a slower, less heavy delivery of water, which causes less damage to, and interference with, the soil. In addition, the lower the spout, the easier it is to apply the water accurately.

Next on my list comes the hoe, and although again there are many different designs, they may be divided into two groups – those you pull towards you (either drawing out a drill or in a drawing, chopping action to control weeds) and those you push, known as Dutch hoes. Ideally you should use the draw hoe for seed drills and to earth up crops like potatoes and the true Dutch hoe to control weeds and leave a nice fine tilth. The draw hoe can be used to control weeds, but you

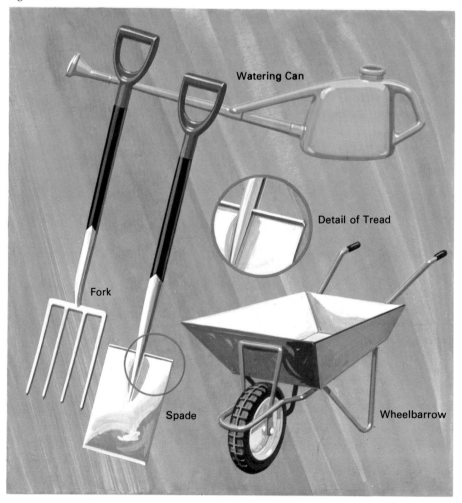

Watering Can

Detail of Tread

Fork

Spade

Wheelbarrow

have to work forward with it which means you not only tread on the soil you have just worked, but in damp soil conditions you will also tread back weeds as well as consolidating some of the newly made tilth.

While the traditional Dutch hoe has the blade supported on a 'Y' frame a number of makes now have either a 'T' or 'L' shaped head. These more recent designs make it possible to get right up to plants for weed control or to thin out seedlings. Care is needed, however, because the outer edges of the hoe will be out of sight under the soil, in a position to easily slip through the plant root by mistake.

Secateurs are useful to all gardeners and the vegetable gardener is no exception. They may be used for prepar-

experience, you need a strong wrist to cope with the longer handle. Hand trowels are usually offered as a pair with small hand forks, but the latter have little use other than on a rockery.

Garden forks come quite low on my priority listing because the spade can be used in most instances and is also more adaptable. If a garden has a large proportion of stones, however, a fork will penetrate the soil more easily than a spade. The fork can also be used as a mixture between rake and cultivator if turned with tines down towards the soil and pulled towards the operator. A good rake would however, be better to prepare a fine level tilth before seed sowing or when filling in seed drills, for example. A long-handled cultivator is also useful on a larger plot

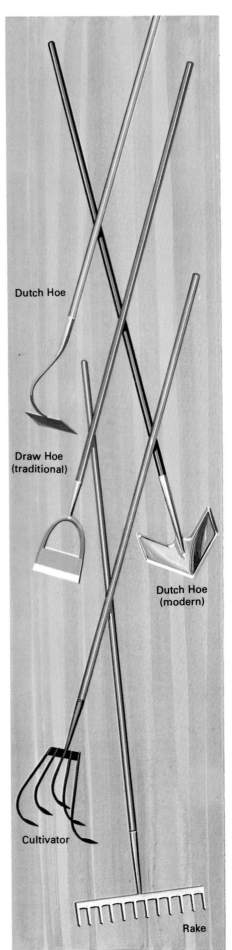

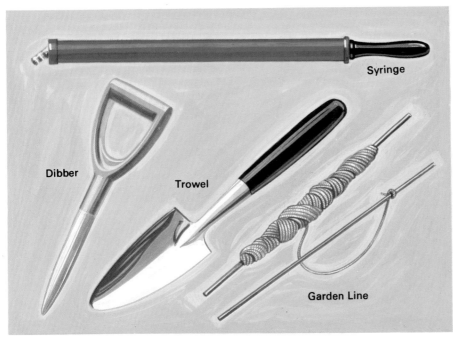

Figure 11.

ing sticks for peas, gathering peppers, marrows and so on. Secateurs with replaceable working parts will give a very long working life and are easily sharpened. Do buy good quality secateurs, cheap designs will very soon lose their edge or become twisted at the axis.

Transplanting
Most vegetable transplanting can be done with a dibber, easily made from an old, broken tool handle, but a trowel will also make things easier for you. Top quality and the highest priced are the stainless steel ones, but whatever price you pay, you have a choice of a short cranked handle design or a long straight handle. In my

where a sizeable area of soil needs regular light surface cultivation.

Other useful pieces of equipment include a light wheelbarrow (with as wide a wheel as possible to make it easier to use on wet soil), a sharp pocket knife and some form of syringe or sprayer for insecticides and fungicides. The relatively cheap plastic hand sprayers will give adequate service for a number of years if used carefully and not abused by dropping or leaving filled during frosty conditions.

Using mechanical cultivators can be one way of reducing the work load, but they can be heavy and difficult to handle. Never rotavate heavy soils when wet.

Figure 12.

Soils and How to Improve Them

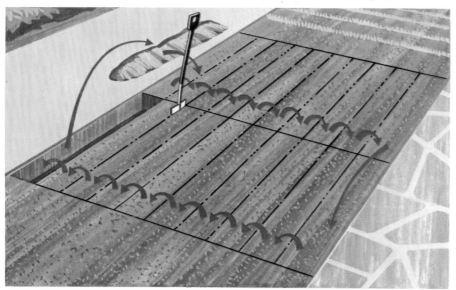

Figure 13: Single digging. There is no need to divide the area on a small plot.

DIGGING THE SOIL

There are four general types of soil – light and sandy; medium loam, (generally referred to as good garden soil); heavy clay; and chalky. All types of soils will be improved by the addition of well rotted animal manure, composted vegetation and peat. Heavy clay soils, for example, become much easier to dig, hoe and rake if you work peat and well rotted compost into them. When you do this, concentrate the application in a small area, spreading a layer 3 in (7·5 cm) deep or so and then cultivating it. When economics allow treat another area and so on, until you have improved the whole plot. Don't scatter a little peat over a big area – this way the real value is lost and you will never see any benefits.

The same advice goes for well rotted organic matter although here the limitations are those imposed by just accommodating and rotting down sufficient waste vegetation, rather than buying the peat. One tip when buying peat, however, is to always purchase by volume, never by weight, which is dependent on the amount of water the peat contains. The lighter coloured peats are less decomposed than the black ones and are therefore likely to last slightly longer in the soil.

Organic matter dug and worked into the soil in whatever form has many functions. It helps light soils retain moisture; it improves the drainage on heavy soils; it tends to reduce or eliminate the extreme alkalinity of chalk soils and it encourages root growth in all soils. You can dig well rotted manure and compost into the soil during the autumn and winter soil preparation, or you can spread it on the surface as a mulch (a blanketing layer of material used to retain moisture and smother weeds) to dig in later. It is not a bad idea to use peat as a mulch along rows of runner beans, brussels sprouts and similar crops, as the peat gives a clean path on which to tread and in wet conditions helps to prevent your shoes getting covered in mud.

Other methods of soil improvement include mixing sand and well weathered ashes into heavy soil to improve drainage qualities and make them easier to work; and adding heavy soil to light, sandy soils which works in a reverse way to improve the water retention of the sand. This is not very easy for the average gardener to achieve, however.

Whatever the soil type some form of annual cultivation is necessary and one of the attractions of vegetable growing for me is the opportunity of burying any mistakes once a year, thus having a perfectly clean start for the next season. Digging need not be the painfully hard job some people make it out to be. The tricks are to use a comfortable spade, (the blade of which should be kept shiny and clean) and not to lift too much soil at a time.

Follow these simple step-by-step digging instructions to prepare your vegetable plot. First take out a trench the width and depth of a spade at one end of the plot (see figure 13). Pile the soil in a heap at the other end. Turn over a 3–4 in (8–10 cm) wide strip of soil, one spade full at a time, across the plot. Move back over the next 3–4 in (8–10 cm) strip, and so on, until you have covered the plot. Use the soil from the first trench to fill the last one. Always lift a smaller spadeful than you think you can manage and take your time.

Put down a layer of peat on wet heavy soils to keep your feet clean and make the digging easier. Bury any short lived weeds (the kinds without thick perennial roots) as you dig but don't miss the chance of picking out any of those thick perennial weed roots as you go. It will save you a lot of hoeing next year (see Weeds and their Control, page 117).

When you are digging in the autumn and early winter, leave the spadefuls of soil in big lumps. The processes of frost cooling the soil and then thawing, rain wetting it and wind drying it out all help to break it down into crumbly pieces. In spring and summer, however, break the soil down as you dig to prevent it drying into

Figure 14: Double digging involves cultivating the lower soil as well as the top soil. It is useful for deep rooted vegetables and crops like runner beans.

 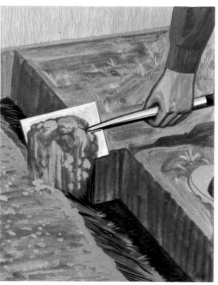 

Figure 15: Don't take too much soil at each spadeful . . .

Figure 16: . . . a smaller amount is easier to lift. Don't hurry digging work.

Figure 17: Leave heavy soils in lumps, the winter weather will break them down.

large lumps and thus losing a lot of moisture. Try to dig when it looks as if you are in for a few hours dry and drying weather. This is particularly important on heavy soils as rain on the freshly dug soil will destroy the crumbly structure you have been working so hard to create.

MANURES

Animal manure is a very good soil improving material, but is best rotted down with other organic matter such as straw, peat and wood shavings before use. Its goodness stems from the fact that it provides the basic plant foods, (also supplied by chemical fertilisers), as well as composted organic matter which improves the physical crumbliness of soil.

You should apply animal manure in moderation, as too much of it, particularly if it is not well rotted down can cause temporary 'scorch' damage to plants. It is fairly unlikely that the average gardener will have too much manure to add, however, and it is well worth remembering that all natural and organic materials, even if added to excess, will do no permanent damage to the soil. This is not the case with chemical fertilisers, if too heavily applied, can damage crops and soils for a number of years. Natural liquid manure can be made by soaking sheep and cattle manure in water – diluted to just colour the water.

The combination of peat and animal manure is 'perfection' for gardeners as it provides plenty of organic material to improve the soil as well as food for the plants. When buying any

form of animal manure, go simply for the greatest bulk you can get for your money. Where manures have been used to grow a previous crop, (for example horse manure and peat used for mushrooms), they remain valuable for the supply of organic matter but will have had the plant foods depleted.

Occasionally the term 'green manuring' is used and it refers to the cultivation of a rapidly growing plant like annual lupin and mustard to produce masses of foliage which is then dug into the soil. The leaves and stems of these plants provide the soil with improving organic matter. Although in fact lupins and similar legumes also add nitrogen to the soil, extra nitrogen fertiliser has to be added when digging in most green manure crops. It should be sprinkled over the land to speed the rotting down process. If it is not applied, the following crop may be starved of this basic plant food. Lawn grasses and clover are excellent green

manures so if you are digging up a piece of old lawn don't discard the turf – instead dig it well into the soil to improve future crops.

COMPOST
Rotted-down Plant Remains
Gardening provides great opportunity to be virtually self-sufficient – a trend currently much in favour. All the goodness taken from the soil by growing vegetable crops can be replaced by rotted down old leaves, stems, lawn mowings and so on which accumulate in the garden. Well rotted down, or 'composted', plant remains are a perfect soil additive, and provide plant food and organic matter to improve the crumbliness of the soil. There are many involved and detailed descriptions of compost making and compost gardening but like everything else, it is really only the general principles you need to remember. The system I like best uses four posts 4 ft (120 cm) long

Figure 18. Large lumps (left) must be broken down, either by the weather or further digging, to provide crumbly textured soil (right) for planting.

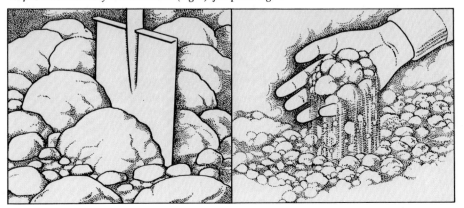

13

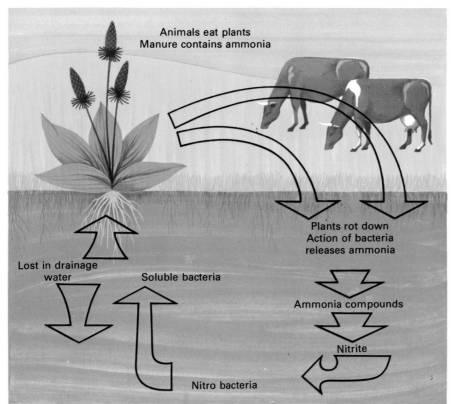

Figure 19: The process of animals grazing and plants growing promotes a perpetual cycle of nitrogen and mineral extraction and replacement in the soil. This 'cycle of life' is of vital importance in the growing of vegetables.

thoroughly mixed with garden waste to enrich the ultimate compost, but keep a look-out for vermin which may be attracted if too much waste food is added to the heap.

FERTILISERS

Nitrogen, phosphates and potash are the three major chemicals supplying plant foods. They can be purchased in natural organic form or as inorganic chemical fertilisers. Nitrogen, the main food in organic dried blood and inorganic sulphate of ammonia, encourages rapid leafy growth and should predominate when applying

Garden-produced compost is of great value to the vegetable grower.

driven 12 in (30 cm) into the soil to mark out a rectangle 5ft × 3 ft (150 cm × 90 cm). Wind wire netting round the stakes to form the compost bin, and line it with polythene. Alternatively use polythene sheet and other materials such as old pieces of board and corrugated sheet to form the sides. You can of course buy and use one of the various factory made compost containers, but obviously the more sophisticated they are, the higher the price will be.

All the non-woody plant remains – pea and bean stalks, cabbage leaves, weeds and lawn mowings, raked up tree leaves and kitchen waste – can all be tipped into the bin. Once you have accumulated a fair heap, pull out the stakes and re-erect the bin on an adjacent site. You can then make a new heap by placing the least well decayed material from the top of the first heap at the bottom of the new one, and so on, until you have completely turned the heap (see figure 20).

Shake the material out a bit as you go because air is needed to speed the decomposition. Two other commodities are needed for the most rapid rotting down – namely moisture, (so have a nearby can of water to use on dry spots as you turn the heap) and some form of nitrogen. If you have

rabbits or similar pets then their hutch cleanings will help provide the nitrogen. If you have no animal manure a good sprinkling of proprietary compost maker may break the self-sufficiency rule but does a really good job!

Start to accumulate rubbish in summer and autumn so as to get a full heap which you can turn early the following spring. It will then rot down fast enough to provide a good site for marrow growing in the summer. After the marrow crop, dig the remaining heap of good friable brown compost into the soil in the autumn. A winter and spring accumulated heap will also be sufficiently rotted down after early summer turning to dig in during the autumn and winter.

Try to mix the waste at all stages as this helps to get the most rapid rotting down. Hard runner bean stalks will rot down more quickly when mixed with lawn mowings, for example, while lawn mowings on their own tend to pack down tightly, excluding air and therefore being slow to decay fully. Beans and other items keep the mowings opened up, and everything rots down more quickly as a result.

Useful organic sources of plant food such as blood from the butcher, fish bones and such like can also be

top dressings to crops like cabbage in spring. Plants which have had a check to growth or those suffering hot dry conditions can be given a new spurt of life with nitrogen-rich fertilisers.

Phosphates, the main constitutent of organic bone meal and inorganic superphosphate, are seldom applied alone except perhaps as a dusting over seed beds. This chemical's main function is to aid root development generally and it also becomes necessary at the seed ripening stage.

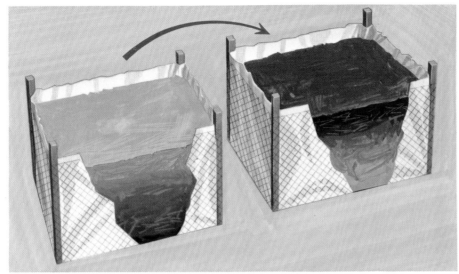

Figure 20: Turning and mixing compost helps to speed the rotting-down process.

Potash, found in wood ash as well as sulphate of potash, is the counter balance to nitrogen. When plants have excessive leaf growth, either from too many moist, warm, sunless days or excess nitrogen, potash will harden up the growth. This helps to make the plant fruitful and improve the flavour of the vegetables.

Compound fertilisers, a mixture of all three, are the easiest to use and are the most frequently bought and applied. The general fertilisers tend to be a balanced mixture of Nitrogen (N), Phosphates (P) and Potash (K), often referred to as NPK. If anything they have an emphasis on nitrogen. Tomato and rose fertilisers, on the other hand, tend to have the emphasis on potash, which gives more flavour to the tomatoes and more colour and greater disease resistance to roses.

Apply a general fertiliser at one handful, 2 oz per square yard, (56 gms per 0·8 sq m) before sowing and planting to increase yields. This will actually do all that most gardeners require but to get even better results, you really need a general fertiliser for initial soil preparation, a higher potash fertiliser for top dressing and one quick acting nitrogen fertiliser like dried blood or nitrate of soda to give plants an occasional 'boost'.

The compound fertilisers are available in dry forms (which may be sprinkled on the surface and hoed in), as well as in soluble form for liquid feeding. Top dressing with dry fertiliser is usually at the lower rate of 1 oz per square yard (28 gms per 0·8 sq m) and you can give more than one application in a season.

Continual cropping and the addi-

tion of compost and manure may make the soil a bit acid and to counteract this apply a dusting of lime in winter to dug soil. Avoid applying too much lime as this will not help growth. The only way of checking the lime content is to test the soil, which you can have done by a specialist or do yourself with a soil testing kit. The figure which indicates the correct amount is pH 6·5. Soils with figures lower than this will need 3 oz lime per square yard (85 gms per 0·8 sq m) or even more to reduce the acidity and raise the pH figure. Lime applied to heavy soils also improves the texture in that it helps the fine clay particles to stick together to form a crumbly structure.

Minor plant foods, often referred to as 'trace elements', include chemicals like magnesium, iron and boron, but as most soils have ample supplies of

these it is seldom necessary to apply them. Very occasionally single crops may not grow well because of the lack of a trace element.

A deficiency of magnesium when growing roses and tomatoes, for example, (indicated by leaves turning yellow between the veins) can be rectified by watering with epsom salts. Cauliflowers which develop narrow leaves (known as 'whiptail') may occur when grown in soils lacking in molybdenum, but the conditions can be eliminated by watering with one dessertspoonful of sodium molybdate in one gallon (4·5 litres) of water per 5 square yards (4 sq m) of soil.

In general, however, a little care in the planning and rotation of crops, coupled with good husbandry in the form of organic matter, such as well rotted compost applied liberally when digging, is all that is needed for good vegetable crops. The addition of a little fertiliser will just increase the yield. The immediately available plant foods are, of course, soluble and taken up by the plant with moisture. Thus it naturally follows that light sandy soils, being free draining, are the most quickly leached, so apply fertilisers little and often on such soils.

Foliar fertilisers are the most quick acting of all – the plant foods in this case being taken up by the leaves. They are either sprayed or watered on to the foliage and will give results in a matter of days if the temperature is warm enough for growth. All leafy crops, roots like carrots and beet, as well as peas and beans, respond to foliar feeding, especially in hot dry weather conditions.

Figure 21: Plants such as marrows grow well on rotted-down compost. Plant two seeds on an average sized heap.

Crop Rotation

It is good, basic gardening practice to rotate crops with one another around a vegetable plot to avoid cropping the same site with the same vegetable or same type of vegetable year after year. Vegetable crops are generally divided into three main groups: root crops, brassicas and the 'others'. The importance of rotation can be demonstrated by taking 'greens' as an example. Greens fall into the brassica group and include broccoli, brussels sprouts, cabbage, cauliflower, kale and savoy. If these crops are grown year after year in the same soil, diseases such as club root will multiply rapidly. If, on the other hand, they are only grown in any one site, one year in three rotated with the other two groups, then the disease is denied its host plant and cannot build up in the soil. The disease club root is a classic example, but the same goes for many diseases and vegetable pests.

Apart from pest and disease, the plant food requirements of the various groups of vegetables are different. The peas and beans, technically called legumes, grow with the help of bacteria which take nitrogen from the air and convert it into nitrogenous plant foods. They do this so efficiently in fact, that they leave more nitrogenous material in the soil after cropping than was there at the outset. Planting brassicas to follow the legumes allows the green vegetables to use this extra nitrogen, thus considerably helping their growth as well as saving the cost of additional nitrogenous fertilisers.

Use of Manure and Compost

Crops such as celery, potatoes and runner beans revel in soils which have plenty of freshly dug in, well rotted animal manure and garden compost. Soils recently enriched in this way are not ideal, however, for root crops such as carrot, chicory and parsnip because the roots tend to divide up and go several ways in search of the manure. It is much better to allow crops like runner beans to take full advantage of the freshly manured land and then follow with carrots a season later. Carrots will grow faster and to a larger size in richer and more moisture retaining soils which contain very well rotted down organic matter.

Although fertilisers can be added to soil at any stage, it is a good idea to apply lime (if it is needed) ahead of brassicas. In a normal rotation scheme this will give the greatest period of time between the application of lime and the planting of potatoes, which are

Potatoes in the root crop section of the author's garden, growing alongside the pea and bean section.

more likely to get their skins marked by the disease scab in alkaline (chalky and lime bearing) soils.

Where gardens are large enough the whole rotation scheme can be expanded by separating peas and beans (the legumes) from the 'other crops' group to give a four-year or four-season rotation. Although the real professionals may work their cropping schemes to this level of perfection, for most of us it is quite sufficient to arrange things so that the same crop is not grown on the same site two years running.

The commonly recommended rotational plans have been worked out over many years and are not only very practical, but also labour saving. Autumn, winter and spring maturing brassicas can often be planted to follow early crops of peas with no more cultivation than hoeing or tickling over the surface of the soil with a fork or spade. If soil is dug as early potatoes are lifted, it only needs knocking down to a fine tilth before the August onion sowing. Two main crops can often be grown, therefore, without thoroughly digging over the whole plot a second time, but it is necessary to keep the surface of the soil well hoed and of a crumbly texture, (particularly avoid trampling over it when wet) to achieve this work saving. It will usually be necessary on all but the lightest soils to dig the ground thoroughly for the third crop.

The rotation system also helps in that it tends to throw up a good area of land which can be dug. Most of the main root crops, for example, require lifting in early autumn to be stored and this land can then be dug in prepara-

Peas and broad beans growing alongside spring cabbage with lettuce and radish grown as an intercrop.

	First Year	Second Year	Third Year
Add compost and/or manure	**OTHER CROPS** Aubergine, Beans, Celery, Leeks, Lettuce, Onions Peas, Peppers, Spinach, Sweet Corn, Tomatoes	Brussels Sprouts, Cabbage, Cauliflower, Kale, Savoy, Sprouting Broccoli Kohl-Rabi, Radish, Swede, Turnip, Turnip grown for green foliage	Artichoke, Jerusalem Beetroot Carrot Chicory Parsnip Potatoes
Add fertiliser	**ROOT CROPS** Artichoke, Jerusalem Beetroot Carrot Chicory Parsnip Potatoes	Aubergine, Beans, Celery, Leeks, Lettuce, Onions Peas, Peppers, Spinach, Sweet Corn, Tomatoes	Brussels Sprouts, Cabbage, Cauliflower, Kale, Savoy, Sprouting Broccoli Kohl-Rabi, Radish, Swede, Turnip, Turnip grown for green foliage
Add fertiliser and lime	**BRASSICAS** Brussels Sprouts, Cabbage, Cauliflower, Kale, Savoy, Sprouting Broccoli Kohl-Rabi, Radish, Swede, Turnip, Turnip grown for green foliage	Artichoke, Jerusalem Beetroot Carrot Chicory Parsnip Potatoes	Aubergine, Beans, Celery, Leeks, Lettuce, Onions Peas, Peppers, Spinach, Sweet Corn, Tomatoes

The above chart gives a suggested crop rotation plan for a three-year period.

tion for the succeeding crop rotation.

It is also possible to get two main crops within one rotational group in a season. For example, early peas can be sown, cropped and cleared in time to plant leeks, which provide a second vegetable in the winter. In place of brussels sprouts, which would be sown March/April and cropped from October to April the next year, an alternative would be a crop of summer cauliflower and spring cabbage.

Crops which need considerable space to allow each plant to grow are generally not suitable for inclusion in the 10 ft × 12 ft (3 m × 4 m) vegetable plot. These include marrows and courgettes, cucumbers, melons and pumpkins and gourds. Cucumbers and melons will in any event grow best in a greenhouse structure of some sort, while marrows, pumpkins etc are ideal plants to grow on a compost heap. Perennial crops like Globe artichokes and asparagus are also best grown outside the plot, as once established they can remain in the same place in the ground for many years.

Spacing and Rotation Charts

The coloured squares included in the 'Growing your own Vegetables' section – pages 40–111, and shown right indicate the group to which the various crops belong, which will help you to plan your crop rotation. Green indicates brassicas, yellow – other crops, brown – root crops and bright orange – perennials. The last group are obviously not included in the crop rotation plan. The measurements within the square refer to the spacings between the plants and rows and wherever possible these have been shown approximately to scale.

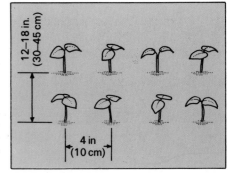

The same spot shown opposite, photographed a few weeks later.

Seed Raising

SEED COMPOST

Good seed germination basically depends on three things – oxygen, moisture and temperature. If there is no oxygen in the growing soil, if there is too much or too little moisture, or if temperatures are too high or too low, the germination of seeds will be erratic. Obviously we have little control over seeds sown outside in the garden, but this is not the case with seeds raised under cover.

The best results will be obtained indoors if the right medium, known as 'compost', is used. Seed compost is used to germinate the seedlings and potting composts are used to grow the seedlings on into larger plants. The word 'compost' used here as a term to describe a growing medium may be somewhat confusing, after having used the same word to describe rotted down vegetable waste for soil improvement.

Seed and potting composts probably get this name from the fact that good turf was cut, stacked and virtually 'composted' before being chopped up and sieved to form the basis of all growing composts in the past. At one time skilled gardeners had many recipes to make growing composts, and they used different ones for nearly every crop. Things are much simpler today, and there is really only one 'recipe' for all seed composts, and one for potting composts. Although John Innes potting composts have a range of fertiliser strengths the basic growing ingredients are the same.

The John Innes Institute did much of the basic research which brought about the reduction in the number of seed raising composts. They were followed by the University of California, who produced the UC mixes, and subsequently several commercial companies. Now one Levington compost for example can be used for nearly all seed raising and plant growing.

Loam-based and Soilless Composts

There is a clear division between John Innes (JI) composts, which are based on steam-sterilised loam (loam being the name for good soil coming from stacked turf) and most other composts, which are soilless. Both give excellent results, but if you have access either to good loam that you can sterilise with steam or ready sterilised loam, then you can make your own 'home' mixes.

John Innes Seed Compost

The ingredients and proportions are as follows:
2 parts by volume loam (sterilised)
1   „   „   „   peat
1   „   „   „   sand
To each 1·28 cu ft or 1 bushel (36 litres) of the mixture is added 1½ oz (42 gms) superphosphate and ¾ oz (20 gms) ground limestone.

John Innes Potting Compost

The ingredients and proportions are as follows:
7 parts by volume loam (sterilised)
3   „   „   „   peat
2   „   „   „   sand
To each 1·28 cu ft or 1 bushel (36 litres), ¾ oz (20 gms) ground limestone and 4 oz (113 gms) John Innes Base fertiliser is added to make JI Potting compost No 1; double the base fertiliser for JI Potting No 2 and 12 oz (340 gms) base fertiliser (×3) for JI Potting no 3.

The base fertiliser is made up of 2 parts hoof and horn meal, 2 parts superphosphate and 1 part sulphate of potash.

The soilless composts are either all peat or a mixture of peat and sand. Mixing base fertilisers into soilless compost is a rather critical operation and it is really better to buy factory mixes than to run the risk of incomplete mixing of trace elements which are needed in the soilless mixes.

It is generally easier to prick off seedlings from the peat-sand than the all-peat composts as the sand gives a finer, more easily separated root. It is therefore not a bad idea to add a little fine, lime-free sand to the all-peat composts if you are using them for seed raising.

Moisture content of composts is important particularly at seed sowing and seedling transplanting stages. For the soil based John Innes compost, moisture content is correct if a handful squeezed in your hand cracks open in one largish crack when you release your grip. If the compost just crumbles when you release the pressure, it is too dry and if the lump remains in the shape of your hand without cracking at all, it is too wet. The peat composts are at the right moisture content if moisture just oozes between your fingers as you squeeze a handful.

Containers just 1 in (2·5 cm) deep can be used for raising many fine seeds, and will use less compost than deeper types.

When transplanting seedlings into new containers, handle by the leaves, not the stem.

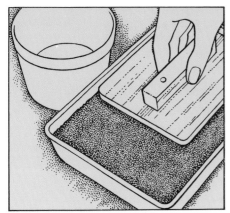

Figure 22: Loosely fill container with compost and firm evenly.

Figure 23: Cover seeds with soil-based compost.

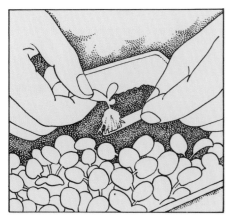

Figure 24. Lift seedlings with stick.

Figure 25. Prick off into boxes.

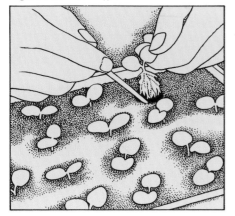

Figure 26: Warmth at the base speeds germination and growth in a simple propagator.

SEED RAISING INDOORS

Raising a few seeds on the window sill can be a profitable occupation with a number of vegetable seeds. Beat the rough winter weather and get a good growing start to the early summer cropping by sowing hardy plants like peas, cabbage, lettuce and cauliflower indoors in January and February to plant out later in cloches. Follow these (still indoors) with the more tender vegetables like cucumbers, peppers, runner beans, sweet corn and tomatoes.

If you have a garden frame or greenhouse, you can considerably increase the number of plants you can raise. There is in any event a limit to the number of plants you will want to have on the window sill and you would be well advised to get a small heated seed propagator for use in all frames and green houses except those heated to 55°–60°F (14–15°C).

Indoor seed raising is however a simple step-by-step operation. Sow small quantities of seeds in flower pots, seed pans, (the equivalent of flower pots but half the depth) and/or seed boxes. Loosely fill the containers to the brim with moistened seed compost, gently firming it with your fingers at first and then using a flat object such as the bottom of another pot or piece of board. This will leave the firmed compost level and about ½ in (1 cm) from the top of the container. (Make sure the corners of boxes are 'finger-firmed' before firming over the whole surface).

Space the seed over the surface and then just cover it with a further layer of seed compost. You can sprinkle the all-peat composts over by hand but you should spread the soil-based composts by passing them through a sieve. Cover the sown containers with glass to help retain moisture and newspaper to exclude light or place them in polythene bags (ideally black ones if they are to stand in the sunlight). A temperature of 55°–65°F (13°–18°C) is needed for speedy germination.

Keep a watch on the sown pots and as soon as you see the first signs of emerging shoots, remove the covers and move the pots close to the glass to give the young seedlings as much light as possible.

As soon as the seedlings are large enough to handle they are ready for spacing out singly in other containers – a practice known as 'pricking off' and 'pricking out'. Use a pointed label or sharpened stick to lift the seedlings up from under the roots and to separate them. Then plant them out singly in pots or space them out in boxes. Always handle seedlings by the leaves, *not* the stem. A damaged leaf will soon be replaced by a new one, but there is only one stem. The earlier you prick off seedlings the less likelihood there is of checks to growth.

Larger seeds like those of broad beans, peas, sweet corn and runner beans can either initially be sown singly in pots or planted two seeds per pot, which are thinned back to one plant as they germinate.

Figure 27: Rake soil to a fine tilth.

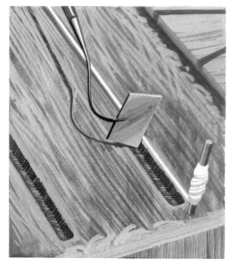

Figure 28: Draw shallow drills for seed.

Figure 29: Space seeds down the drill.

Figure 30: Thin seedlings as recommended.

SEED RAISING – OUTDOORS

A nice crumbly soil is the key to easy and successful outdoor vegetable seed raising. Winter frosts break down autumn and winter dug soils, so they automatically form this required crumbly structure – called tilth – in spring. If you have lumpy, hard soil, however, try mixing a good layer of well moistened peat in with the surface soil. This helps to produce reasonable seed sowing conditions.

When you are preparing the ground for actual sowing, knock down all dug soils with a cultivator, fork or spade and tread along the line of the row once with your feet to firm. Finally level the soil with a rake or spade or achieve the desired tilth.

When the soil is prepared stretch a garden line across the plot to mark out the position of the row and then make the seed drill with a draw hoe, dibber or piece of wood. If the soil is very wet

stand on a board to prevent pressing the soil down hard with your feet.

The depth of drill may vary but most seeds require a drill no more than 1 in (2·5 cm) deep. In practical terms this means sufficient depth to cover the seeds well with soil after sowing. The seed must then be spaced down the drill, and this is best done by sprinkling it along the row from between your fingers. Hold the supply of seed in the palm of your hand and feed it through your thumb and forefinger, to roll the seed into the drill. Alternatively, take a pinch of seed and sprinkle it into the drill.

Cover the seed with soil by shuffling down the row with a foot on each side of the row. Finally firm the soil either by gently treading once or using the back of the rake. Then 'scuffle' the surface to remove footprints and ruffle any smoothed areas which will otherwise go hard after a fall of rain.

Large seeds like broad beans, runner beans and sweet corn can be sown by making a single hole for each seed with a dibber and covering them as you go along. When sowing slow-to-germinate seeds such as onion, parsnip, and parsley, it is worth mixing a little fast germinating seed such as radish or lettuce in with it. These will grow quickly and indicate where the other crops will follow. It also allows you to hoe between the rows to control weeds without disturbing the emerging vegetable seedling. Radish and lettuce, used in this way, are known as indicator crops.

Once the seedlings are through you must thin them out to the spacings recommended for each crop. All seedlings that are left to grow too thickly and too many together – from radish to cauliflower, carrot to lettuce – will be too small to be of use. It is generally a wise precaution to thin out twice, the first time to one half the required distance and then subsequently to the final distance. If slugs, birds and other pests damage a few seedlings, with the two-stage thinning there is a fifty-fifty chance they will take unwanted seedlings. Some vegetables, like carrots, will in fact provide small but harvestable roots at the second thinning.

Sparrows can play havoc with young seedlings, not only lettuce, which is possibly the worst affected, but also peas, beetroot and many others. If you cannot protect the emerging seedlings with cloches, place a stick every 3–4 ft (90–120 cm) down the row and twine a few strands of black cotton 2–3 in (5–8 cm) above

Planting Broad Bean seeds.

Figure 31: Protect young seedlings with lines of thread.

the seedlings to discourage birds.

Quite apart from protection from birds, cloches are most valuable for seed raising. Placed over the soil a week or two before sowing, they will dry and warm the soil which makes tilth formation easier and helps germination. They also protect fine tilth from damage caused by heavy rain.

SEED GERMINATION CHART

There are often too many seeds in one packet to sow in a small plot, so every now and then you will find you have seed left over from previous years. This chart will show whether it is worth sowing left-over seeds in subsequent years. However, if in doubt it is better to use fresh seed than risk the chance of a crop failure.

The figures given in the chart can only be a guide because seed life depends very much on harvesting and storage conditions. Sun, warmth and dry harvesting conditions invariably give top quality seed which has a longer storage life. Cool, damp harvesting conditions are likely to give poorer quality seed with a correspondingly shorter storage life.

Dry conditions and an even temperature are the best storage conditions for long seed germination life. They can be produced most easily by using an airtight container, such as a biscuit tin or screw top jar with a small sachet of silica gel placed inside to keep the atmosphere dry. The back of a damp shed or shelf in the greenhouse where temperatures rocket and then fall as quickly are *not* good storage places.

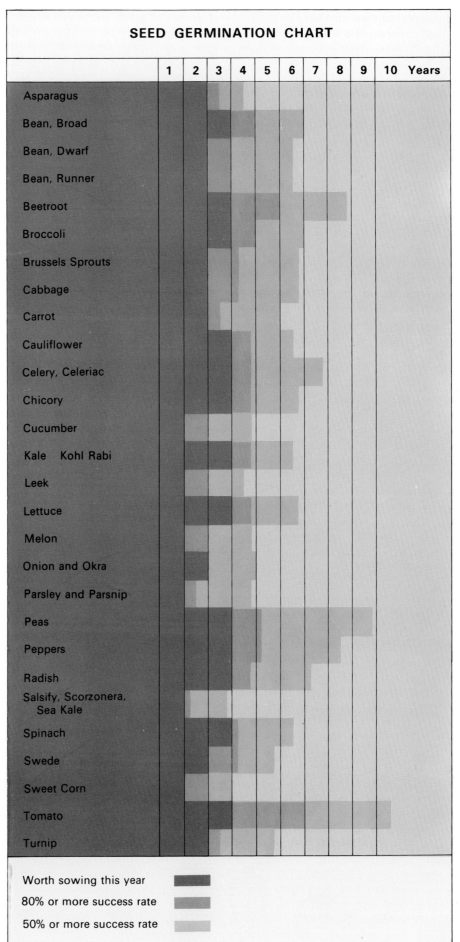

SEED GERMINATION CHART

Worth sowing this year

80% or more success rate

50% or more success rate

The 10ft x 12ft (3m x 4m) Vegetable Plot

Gardening on a small scale is the easy way to have all the benefits and satisfaction from growing plants with the minimum of work. Growing your own vegetables also gives garden-fresh food of better quality and flavour as well as saving you money.

Both the newcomer to gardening and the skilled gardener who is used to cropping very large plots need have no fears about operating on what may appear to be a miniature scale. Although the choice of the rectangular dimension at the outset was no more than a convenient size and shape for a television screen and could be accommodated in the studio situation, in practice, the 10 ft × 12 ft (3 m × 4 m) rectangle has proved ideal.

Dividing the plot up into three sections for rotation purposes is easy and the 10 ft (3 m) long rows are sufficient to provide a reasonable gathering at any one time of all the vegetables grown. Surrounding the plot by grassed, paved or concreted paths gives easy access, even in wet conditions, and makes it possible to do a good part of the cultural and harvesting operations from the side paths. This keeps your feet clean and avoids treading down the soil or trekking soil indoors with you. If you stand alternately on either side of the plot, you will find it is possible to hoe from the middle to the side without putting a foot on the soil. Most of the vegetables can be harvested from the side, so it is really only when you are digging, sowing and doing some planting that it is necessary to actually tread over the plot.

As gardening is still in the province

Vegetables in the plot: from l. to r. sweet corn, runner beans, beetroot, lettuce as an indicator crop, carrots, onions and peas.

Figure 32: The vegetable plot in late summer. Note cabbage planted to mature in succession.

22

of the 'artist' as well as the 'scientist', there are no unbreakable rules! While the 10 ft × 12 ft (3 m × 4 m) plans are particularly suited to many requirements, there is nothing to stop you reducing the size even further should you so wish.

Our plans are designed to provide at least sufficient of any one vegetable at a gathering to provide a serving for four people. If you need bigger servings and more vegetables then you could cultivate two or more plots simultaneously. Beware of attempting to produce great quantities, however, as you are likely to achieve the maximum returns when you cultivate one 10 ft × 12 ft (3 m × 4 m) plot really well and intensively rather than two less efficiently. Once you have the one under control and you really know what you are doing, extension is easy and more likely to be successful.

Figure 33: Crop rotation demonstrated on the plot from l. to r. – Other crops, root crops and brassicas.

The practical demonstrations of small plot vegetable growing on television have also proved that it is possible to cultivate our basic crop plan spending no more than one hour per week and, in the extreme case, also strictly limiting the money spent both on seeds and other sundry gardening items. Choice of vegetables has been geared to providing a year-round supply, rather than a glut of crops at one time of the year. It also proved that one need not worry too much about soil, as it was necessary to use the soil within reach of the television cameras. After the first spade or two of digging the site looked almost undiggable, being more grassed-over rubbish than soil! Persevering with the digging, how-

ever, proved it was more than possible to grow good vegetables. The criterion would seem to be, if you can dig it – that appears to be good enough! A small area can also be quickly improved by adding well rotted compost and other organic matter.

BASIC PLAN
This cropping plan is very simple to carry out but achieves all the objectives, so far discussed – that is, rows which are long enough to give yields at one gathering to serve four people, less than one hour per week spent on cultivating the plot and the provision of freshly grown vegetables to eat any week of the year.

Our aim has been to get everything possible from the vegetable plot, but if, for example, your family does not like or does not want peas, all you need to do is look for the same rotation coloured squares in the vegetable section (pages 42–111), to find an alternative

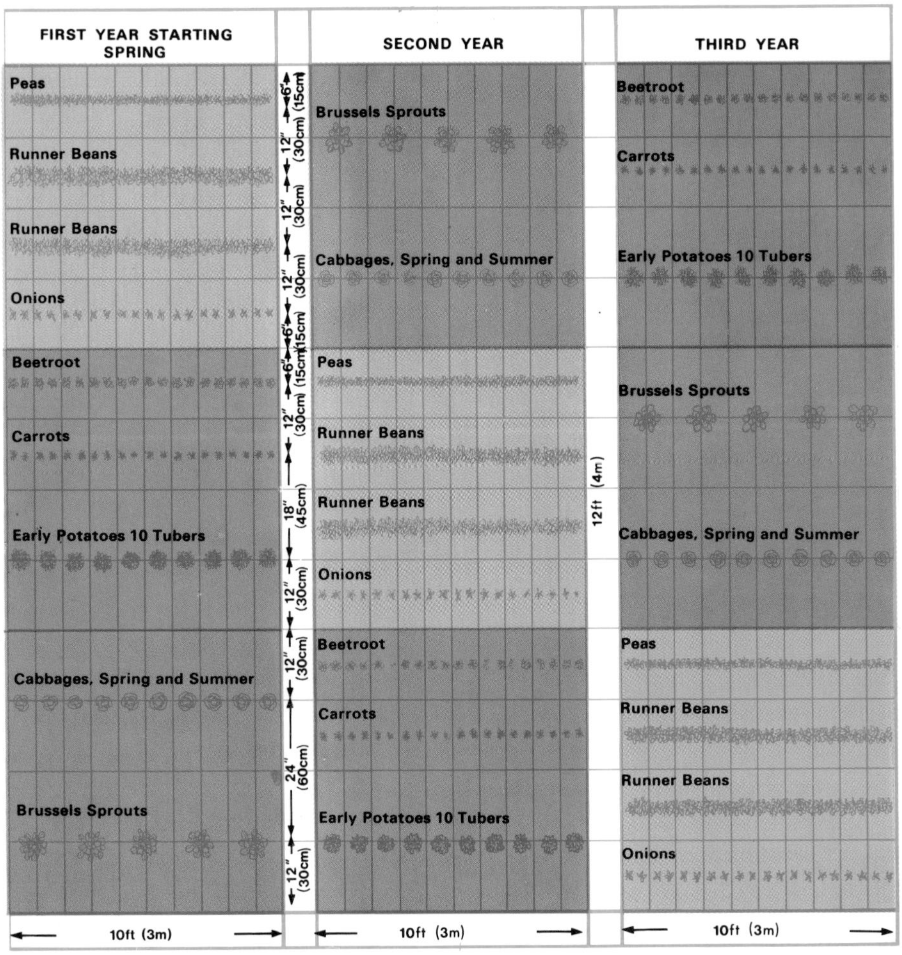
FIRST YEAR STARTING SPRING
SECOND YEAR
THIRD YEAR
Peas
Runner Beans
Runner Beans
Onions
Beetroot
Carrots
Early Potatoes 10 Tubers
Cabbages, Spring and Summer
Brussels Sprouts
Brussels Sprouts
Cabbages, Spring and Summer
Peas
Runner Beans
Runner Beans
Onions
Beetroot
Carrots
Early Potatoes 10 Tubers
Beetroot
Carrots
Early Potatoes 10 Tubers
Brussels Sprouts
Cabbages, Spring and Summer
Peas
Runner Beans
Runner Beans
Onions
6" (15cm)
12" (30cm)
12" (30cm)
12" (30cm)
6" (15cm)
6" (15cm)
12" (30cm)
18" (45cm)
12" (30cm)
12" (30cm)
24" (60cm)
12" (30cm)
12ft (4m)
10ft (3m)
10ft (3m)
10ft (3m)

Figure 34: Rotation Guide for the Basic Plan.

crop to peas. You can then adjust the row spacing accordingly.

Working systematically down the crops in plan order (see figure 34) I will give brief notes on the cultural needs and crop timings. Full details for each crop will be found in the vegetable section (pages 42–111).

Peas: Sow in the plot in October, November and March to June or in pots indoors January/February to plant out in February/March. Early sowings maybe harvested in June and brussels sprouts sown immediately.

Runner beans: Sow indoors in late April to plant out after the chance of frost, or sow directly in the plot in May. Choose dwarf varieties of runner beans or dwarf french beans if you don't want to erect supports for tall-growing runner beans. The runners will crop well from July to September.

Onions: Push the small sets gently into the soil in March/April to give good bulbs in August/September. These can be stored for use from October to June. Sow a sprinkling of salad onion seed along the row, either in the previous September or at planting time to provide salad onions in the spring and summer respectively.

Beetroot: Sow any time from April to June to give roots from July to October. The roots can be cooked fresh, stored for use from October to May and/or pickled.

Carrots: Sow from March to June to provide fresh-pulled roots as well as roots to store for winter and spring use.

Potatoes: This crop takes up quite a lot of room and replacing it with carrots, parsnips or other root vegetables would possibly give a better return. However, most people would make a sacrifice in order to have freshly dug new potatoes from the garden! To get the maximum yield put the ten tubers in a tray on a light window-sill in early spring. This encourages the production of short dark green shoots and gives subsequent earlier and heavier yields. Plant the tubers in April to lift in July/August. Lifting the potatoes in good time clears the soil ready for the next season's sowing of spring onions for salad, and perhaps a row of overwintered lettuce (which will be cleared before the second year's runner beans need the space).

Cabbage: Sow in July/August to provide plants to set out in September and either cut as 'greens' in late winter/early spring or as single cabbages in spring. You can plant a second sowing of summer maturing cabbage once you have cleared the spring cabbage. Alternatively, if you cut the spring cabbage leaving the stump and a few leaves behind, the stump will produce a second crop of small cabbage.

Brussels sprouts: Sow the seed in February/March and plant out in May/June. Earlier sowing and planting and the use of early varieties will give early sprouts (in October/December), ensuring the land is cleared in time for the spring planting of potatoes in the second year. Don't forget that new shoots from the old brussels stems make delicious 'spring greens'. Grow radish intercrops on each side of the brussels.

HARVEST CHART FOR 10 ft×12 ft (3×4 m) VEG PLOT

Vegetable	Jan	Feb	Mar	Apr	May	Jun	Jul	Aug	Sep	Oct	Nov	Dec
Peas						●	●					
Lettuce					●	●						
Beans							●	●	●			
Onions	○	○	○	○	○			●	●	● ○	○	○
Onion Salad			●	●	●	●	●					
Beetroot	○	○	○	○	○		●	●	●	● ○	○	○
Carrots	○	○	○	○	○		●	●	●	● ○	○	○
Potatoes	○	○	○	○	○		●	●	●	● ○	○	○
Cabbage	●	●	●	●	●	●	●	●	●	●	●	●
Brussels Sprouts	●	●	●						●	●	●	●
Radish						●	●	●				

● ● ● Harvesting ○ ○ ○ Freeze/Store

THE BASIC PLAN SIMPLIFIED

The basic plan is geared to year-round crops and a reasonable range of vegetables, but it is possible to get bigger returns for your money and efforts if you reduce the range of vegetables you grow and if you don't necessarily want to achieve maximum year-round cropping. It could be for example, that you would like to grow as many beans or peas as possible to put in the deep freeze for winter use.

If you intend to use your plot this way you will still need to rotate the crops, so as to avoid growing one crop in the same soil year after year. Taking the most simple system, which would be to grow just one kind of vegetable in the 10 ft × 12 ft (3 m × 4 m) plot in any one year, you could actually grow about 210–250 lettuce in two crops! (The greater number would be achieved by growing compact varieties like 'Little Gem', 'Tom Thumb' and 'Winter Density'). Intensive cropping with just lettuce is not really practical for most families, however, because the crop will tend to come in gluts – and there will be far too much to cope with at one time. If you have put the whole plot down to peas or runner beans, then a deep freezer would accommodate the yield providing you have time to pick and prepare all the crop for freezing, remembering it will all be ready at one time.

Dividing the plot into three sections as already suggested and cropping each section with a vegetable from a different crop rotation group is an easier and more acceptable choice for the average home gardener. Take, for example, lettuce, beans and cabbages: all are easy to grow, all are popular and all yield well under a wide range of soil and climatic conditions.

Where fewer varieties are grown,

FIRST YEAR STARTING SPRING	SECOND YEAR	THIRD YEAR
Lettuce		Spring Cabbages
Lettuce	Runner Beans Double Row Caned	
Lettuce	Peas	Spring Cabbages
Lettuce	Runner Beans, Pinched	Spring Cabbages
Runner Beans Double Row Caned	Chicory	Lettuce
	Chicory	Lettuce
Peas	Chicory	Lettuce
Runner Beans, Pinched	Chicory	Lettuce
Cabbages Summer	Lettuce	
Cabbages Summer	Lettuce	Runner Beans Double Row Caned
	Lettuce	Peas
Cabbages Summer	Lettuce	Runner Beans, Pinched
← 10ft (3m) →	← 10ft (3m) →	← 10ft (3m) →

Figure 35: Rotation Guide for the Basic Plan Simplified.

providing greater yields, the need for some form of storage is usually necessary. To take again the example of beans grown as a major part of the proposed cropping plan, for freeze storing, then spinach and sweet corn are two very complementary crops. Sweet corn grows much better in blocks than in single rows and a 10 ft × 4 ft (3 m × 1·2 m) section will take four rows of the dwarf varieties which could provide as many as 40 cobs.

Figure 36: Crops as they appear in the second year of the above chart.

Winter salads are much in demand and often quite highly priced in the shops. It is not practical for most gardeners to grow lettuce to harvest in the middle of winter because heated greenhouse conditions are needed to harvest at this time. Where a root crop is needed to help with the rotation, however, then chicory can be sown in one third of the plot alongside lettuce – the lettuce will provide salads from May to November, and the chicory roots (lifted in October, stored and a few brought from store every ten to fourteen days to force (see page 67)) provide salad leaves from December to April.

Intercropping can also be introduced without complicating the three main crops too much. For example, you can sow rows of radish between cabbage and lettuce, or spinach before and between rows of sweet corn. If you are a complete newcomer to gardening, begin with the three simple crops plan – one in each third of the plot – and once these are growing well, introduce one or two intercrops. After that you can move on to the eight to ten crops in the basic plan.

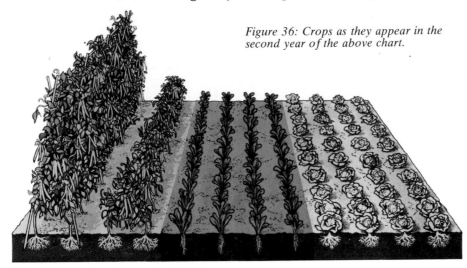

ADDITIONS TO THE BASIC PLAN

To get the maximum yield from the small vegetable plot, all the ground space should be covered with foliage, but when you start vegetable growing, you will soon discover that even main crops like potatoes and brussels sprouts do not fully cover the ground with their foliage all the year round. All plants need just enough space to keep their natural leaf spread exposed to sunlight. With this in mind, you can get the maximum from your plot by even more careful planning, and fitting in extra crops wherever and whenever space allows.

There are many ways of intensifying the basic cropping plan and the following suggestions should give you some ideas. Firstly it is possible to plant lettuce raised indoors on each side of a row of peas sown under cloches in March. Quick maturing lettuce (varieties like 'Tom Thumb') will be cut before peas and runner beans need the space. Also, if you water the row of peas very well just before the pods are ready to pick, it not only helps to swell the pods and increase the yield but softens the ground sufficiently to allow another lot of seed to be pushed in beside the old row. The new seedlings develop as the old crop dies down, so you gather two rows of peas in the year.

You can have an overwintered crop of spring salad onions growing between beetroot and carrots. Lifting the beetroot and carrot as early as possible allows time for a second sowing of these crops too. Another choice would

An intercrop of lettuce grown between rows of peas, sown in succession.

be to mix parsnip and early carrot, and then pull all the carrots at the second thinning, leaving only the parsnips to develop. You can lift potatoes in July and clear the ground to allow sowings of three more rows of carrot, beetroot or spinach. Where the weather is warm and damp it may even be possible to snatch a quick intercrop of spinach from between beetroot and carrots, or carrots and potatoes.

You can grow a number of rows of radish in the 'greens' (brassica) rotation area as an intercrop. In addition to this, you could also crop two rows of turnips on each side of the row of brussels sprouts. Alternatively you could

follow the spring cabbage with two rows of turnips instead of following summer cabbage with spring cabbage.

If cropping is intensified to the maximum you must make full use of pot raised plants. Sweet corn raised indoors in pots, for example, can be kept growing in the pots while spring cabbages mature and are cut. You will then need to hoe the ground immediately and plant out your very well established sweet corn plants. It is this sort of intensification that allows you to get the maximum output for your labours – one good digging of the plot, say for peas, and you can get two pea crops plus a lettuce crop.

Figure 37: Rotation Guide for Additions to the Basic Plan.

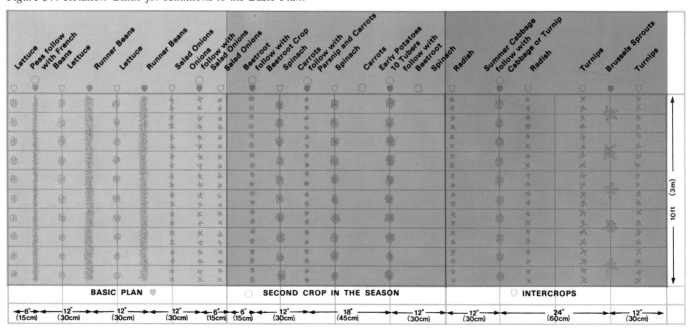

UNUSUAL VEGETABLE PLAN

Ease of travel to other countries and the increased number of foreign restaurants have contributed to the fact that people are becoming much more adventurous in the kinds of vegetables they eat. There is no reason why some of the more unusual vegetables should not be grown in the garden and so we have developed crop plans for vegetables which are just a bit out of the ordinary. The basic plan for growing these is shown in figure 38.

Remember, the spacing distances have been cut to the absolute minimum so as to get in as many crops as possible and produce the maximum output from the 10 ft × 12 ft (3 m × 4 m) plot. The same three-year rotation scheme should be followed for each group and in several cases it is possible to get two crops from the one vegetable type in a year.

Again, full cultural instructions are given for these vegetables in the vegetable growing section from pages 42–111, but working down the suggested crops in plan order here are one or two cultural points:

Peas: It will be necessary to make an early sowing of either Sugar Podded peas, or Petit Pois, if you are to get in the second crop of Asparagus peas. A full crop of Asparagus peas will depend on a warm autumn.

Beans: Sow the dwarf varieties of broad beans which are much more compact and have upright pods. They are particularly suitable for the small plot. It is said you can pick the very young pods of broad beans and cook them whole, like the Sugar Podded peas, and if this is to your taste it will certainly clear the broad beans in time for a second crop of dwarf beans! You can choose from various yellow, purple striped and purple podded kinds, although all coloured podded types turn green when cooked.

Shallots: One of the easiest of all crops to grow and if pulled early and eaten green in May/June, you will be able to clear the soil in time to grow a crop of Florence fennel. Garlic can be grown as an alternative to shallots (to get the best skin finish on the garlic, cover with a polythene tunnel in August).

Carrot: Try one of the unusual root shapes of carrot or the winter stored root crop, scorzonera. Although the round carrots have a good flavour they

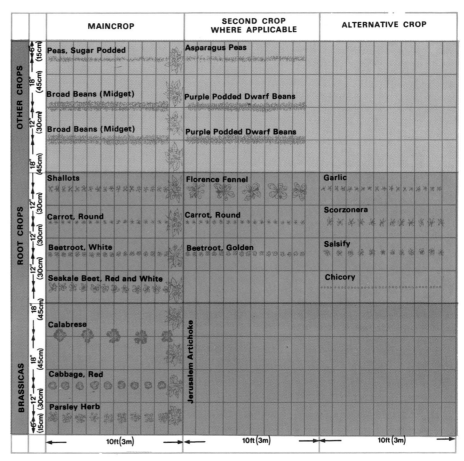

Figure 38: Rotation Guide for Unusual Vegetable Plan.

are perhaps less easy to prepare unless you have equipment similar to mechanical potato peelers.

Beet: It is the unusual colours of white and golden beetroot which prompts this selection, but if you are not keen on beetroot or the spinach-like leaves of golden beet, then you could substitute the 'vegetable oyster', salsify.

Purple-podded beans make an interesting vegetable to grow for a change.

Seakale beet: The broad leaf stalks of seakale beet are an excellent substitute for the tender forced shoots of seakale. An alternative crop if this is not to your liking could be chicory which provides roots to lift in October to store and force through the winter. These provide salad leaves from December to April

Brassicas: There are several less common green vegetables which can be grown, from the sprouting kale 'Pentland Brig' to purple cauliflowers. Our plan features calabrese, which is useful for deep freezing and much easier to grow than cauliflower, and the red cabbage which may be cooked as a fresh vegetable and pickled. Recently introduced varieties of red cabbage are more compact and will stand the closer spacing.

The plan also allows an edging of herbs along one end of the plot where you could grow parsley, chives, thyme, mint and sage.

One final suggestion is to plant a single row of Jerusalem artichokes along the northern or western edge. This gives a little wind protection to the other crops and also provides a crop of winter tubers.

Vegetable	Seed cost	Proportion of seed used	Value of vegetables produced
Peas	13p	6½p	.75p
Lettuce	9p	4½p	2.25p
Runner beans	16p	8p	1.60p
Onions – sets	4p	4p	45p
Onions – seed	7p	4p	30p
Beetroot	20p	10p	48p
*Carrot	7p	3½p	30p
Potatoes 10 tubers	20p	20p	1.00p
*Brussels sprouts	20p	5p	10p
Cabbage	7p	2½p	1.00p
Radish	5p	5p	.95p
Sweet Corn	9p	4½p	1.40p
	£1.37p	77½p	£10.58p

What you get for your money.

VALUE FOR MONEY – VEGETABLE GROWING ON ANY SCALE

The original 10 ft × 12 ft (3 m × 4 m) plot cropping was tested in 1974 and 1975 when the basic price for the ordinary pictorial packets of vegetable seeds was from 5–9p per packet. Some two years later seed prices had almost doubled and the consumer prices of fresh and frozen vegetables had shown comparative increases in most cases.

The value for money of growing one's own fresh vegetables was clearly proven then and the principle continues. Although the cost of seeds and gardening sundries will fluctuate it is almost certain they will remain comparatively in the same price order as shop-bought fresh vegetables. The figures here just need multiplying up or down to relate to current costs for an up-to-date cash appraisal.

The cost of seeds left 22½p for the purchase of slug pellets and a little liquid fertiliser for the runner beans to round up the expenditure to £1. It will be seen that the yields gave a 10-fold return on the cash invested. The crops marked * were very poor in the year that these actual figures were recorded. Hot, dry weather caused the poor brussels sprout and carrot crop, and pigeons also damaged the brussels. It is likely, however, that every year will see a problem of some kind – one or two vegetables may be very cheap in the shops or climatic conditions may reduce your own yield in some cases.

The seed bill could be reduced to some extent, by, for example, sowing some of your own runner bean seeds from the previous year's crop, or by growing shallots and saving a few planting sets for the next season, instead of buying onion sets.

The cost and return on growing two crops from seed to cover the whole 10 ft × 12 ft (3 m × 4 m) plot is shown below. Although these figures were estimated in 1974, since when actual prices will have risen, the proportion of outlay to return on investment remains the same.

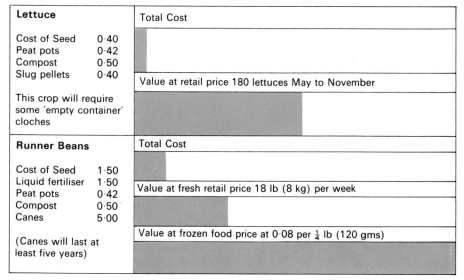

Lettuce		Total Cost
Cost of Seed	0·40	
Peat pots	0·42	
Compost	0·50	
Slug pellets	0·40	
This crop will require some 'empty container' cloches		Value at retail price 180 lettuces May to November
Runner Beans		Total Cost
Cost of Seed	1·50	
Liquid fertiliser	1·50	Value at fresh retail price 18 lb (8 kg) per week
Peat pots	0·42	
Compost	0·50	
Canes	5·00	
(Canes will last at least five years)		Value at frozen food price at 0·08 per ¼ lb (120 gms)

CLIMATE

A number of fairly popular vegetable crops that can be grown in the average garden are nevertheless not hardy and will die if subjected to a degree or two of frost. Unfortunately the rather unpredictable British climate makes it difficult to give exact and specific sowing and planting dates, but some general guides can be given.

With a crop such as potatoes, for example, the gamble of early planting is not as great as it would be with an early sowing of runner beans. The potatoes will take several weeks after planting to develop roots and for the shoots to grow above the surface, whereupon any frost would only damage the shoot growth above the ground. Although growth would be checked and the yield of tubers both reduced and delayed as a result, new shoots would still be produced from below ground to carry a crop. On the other hand, if emerging runner bean seedlings are damaged by frost there would be virtually no chance of recov-

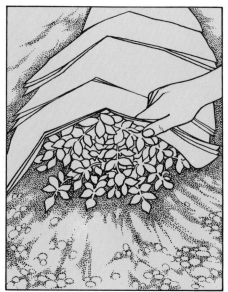

Figure 39: Cover tender foliage with newspaper to protect it on frosty nights.

ery and you would have to sow again to get any crop.

The earlier you sow or plant, the earlier the crop will be ready, comparatively speaking, but if you make your moves too early – when heavy frosts are still likely – then the chance of total failure and the need to start again can occur. The gamble of going for early crops is easy to see – the earlier you start the longer the odds against a 'big win'. There are crops, like tomato, where it is wise to plant a little on the

Figure 40: Water with cold water to aid recovery from radiation frost damage.

late side, producing plants which grow rapidly with no check to growth, rather than plant too early, resulting in the young seedlings receiving a check from cold. This will ultimately delay growth more than the later planting.

Throughout this book, I have given instructions to plant out after the chance of frost has passed. The accompanying map which shows the meteorological average dates for the last likely frost in spring will help you to determine safe planting dates. Remember it will also be necessary to protect ripening half-hardy crops in the autumn before frost occurs.

Other Factors

The warming effect of the Gulf Stream round the western coasts can be seen from the map and it should also be noted that the coastal areas are all milder than inland areas. In addition there are two other factors which help the early planting gambler. The first occurs in the centre of cities where the density of living gives a marked warming effect, making early planting more likely to be successful. The second is the fact that cold air sinks, so gardens on high ground, although affected by wind, are less likely to be affected by frost. Sinking cold air is, of course, a two-edged sword and if your garden is in the bottom of a hollow then cold frosty air is likely to descend and accumulate making frost damage more likely.

You can reduce possible damage from spring frost at night on half-hardy plants, such as potatoes, runner and french beans, by covering the tender foliage of crops with newspaper,

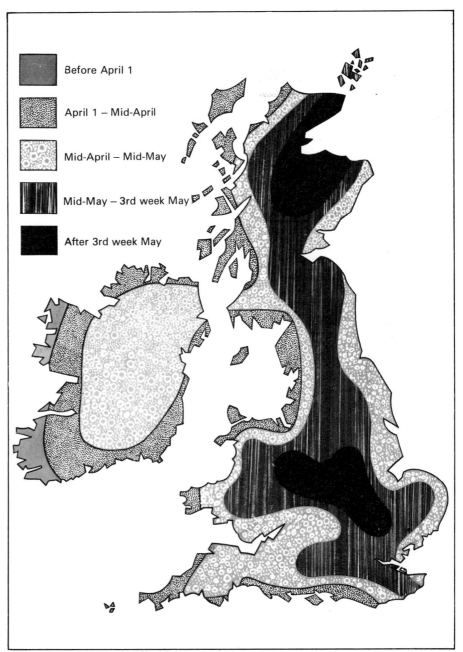

Before April 1

April 1 – Mid-April

Mid-April – Mid-May

Mid-May – 3rd week May

After 3rd week May

Figure 41: Map to show average dates of last frost in spring.

old curtains or similar material until mid-morning. Such covering traps the warmth held in the soil and will reduce the effect of what are called radiation frosts.

Two other things to remember are that rapid thawing out aggravates frost damage – so, in the event of frost, protect plants from early morning sun to allow very slow thawing – and watering with cold water is a help to the recovery from radiation frost damage. Never water with warm water as this causes rapid thawing in the same way as the early morning sun and so increases the chance of damage.

Where vegetable crops, like lettuce, are sown outdoors in the autumn to 'overwinter where climatic conditions

allow', this really refers to degrees of frost to be withstood through the winter. Our last spring frost map is of some help here because the latest areas are also likely to be coldest in winter. If the winter is milder than the general average, it is likely that overwintered crops will survive in virtually all parts of the country. The colder your particular area, then the greater the gamble you will take by sowing seedlings to overwinter. On the other hand, the odds are favourable wherever you live, from the point of view that if the seedlings are lost there is still time to either sow indoors and transplant or sow again in spring. Overwintered crops that survive will give early crops and heavy yields.

Sowing and Harvesting Chart

How to use the chart

When starting to grow vegetables for the first time and at the beginning of each new year it is a help to measure up the plot available and work out where all the different kinds of vegetables you would like to grow will fit. Remember you should rotate the crops so as to avoid having one crop in the same position for several years.

It will be necessary to know when each crop will start to require space and when it will be harvested and this information is given on the chart. So, for example, if you wish to grow peas and brussels sprouts, you can see that peas sown in March will be cleared in July, in time to make way for the brussels sprouts plants. This example would also fit conveniently into the basic crop rotation scheme (see page 17), as the vegetable · pea belongs to the 'other crop' category, while the brussels sprout is a member of the brassica group of vegetables.

Apart from initial crop-planning this chart is also valuable at any time of the year as space becomes available in your vegetable plot. If, for example, you have some space in July, running your finger down the sow-outdoors column will show you that you could start off spring cabbage, lettuce, radish, spinach and turnip. Remember the weather conditions can affect crop maturity by a week or so either way.

WHEN TO SOW, PLANT AND HARVEST

Vegetable	Sow outdoors	Sow outdoors under cloches	Sow indoors	Thin	Transplant outdoors	Jan	Feb	Mar	Apr	May	Jun	Jul	Aug	Sep	Oct	Nov	Dec
Artichoke (Globe)	Perennial				April						●	●	●	●	●		
Artichoke (Jerusalem)	Perennial				Autumn or Spring	○	○	○	○	○	○	○		●	●	○	○
Asparagus	Perennial				April					●	●	●					
Aubergines	—	—	April	—	June								●	●	●		
Beans (broad)	October	—	—	—	—						●	●	●				
Beans (broad) (a)	—	—	(a) Jan/Feb	—	(a) March						●	●	●				
(b)	Mar/Apr	—	—	—	—							●	●				
Beans (French)	June	May	—	—	—							●	●	●			
Beans (runner)	May/June	April	—	—	—							●	●	●	●		
Beetroot	April/June	—	—	May/Jul	—	○	○	○	○	○	●	●	●	●	○	○	○
Broccoli (sprouting)	Apr/May	—	—	—	July/Aug			●	●	●							
Brussels Sprouts	Mar/May	—	—	May/Jun	Jun/Jul	●	●	●	●	●				●	●	●	●
Cabbage (spring)	End July	—	—	—	Sept/Oct			●	●	●	●						
Cabbage (spring)	Early Aug	—	—	Sept	—			●	●	●	●						
Cabbage (summer)	—	—	Feb	—	April						●	●	●	●			
Cabbage (summer)	April	—	—	May	—								●	●	●		
Cabbage (winter)	May	—	—	—	July	●	●	●	●	●						●	●
Cabbage (Savoy)	Mar/April	—	—	—	Jul/Aug	●	●										●
Calabrese	Apr/May	—	—	June	—								●	●	●		
Carrot	Mar/May	—	—	May/June	—	○	○	○	○	○	●	●	●	●	●	○	○
Cauliflower (summer)	Feb/April	—	—	Apr/May	—						●	●					
Cauliflower (summer)(a)	—	Sept	—	—	Mar						●	●					
Cauliflower (summer)(b)	—	—	(b) Jan/Feb	—	Mar						●	●					
Cauliflower (autumn)	Apr/May	—	—	—	Jun/Jul										●	●	
Cauliflower (winter)	May	—	—	—	Jul/Aug				●	●							
Celery	—	—	Mar/Apr	—	May/Jun	●									●	●	●

30

Vegetable	Sow outdoors	Sow outdoors under cloches	Sow indoors	Thin	Transplant outdoors	Jan	Feb	Mar	Apr	May	Jun	Jul	Aug	Sep	Oct	Nov	Dec
Celery (self-blanching)	—	—	Feb/Apr	—	Apr/Jun								●	●	●		
Chicory	Apr/May	—	—	June	—	○	○	○								○	○
Courgette	—	—	Apr/May	—	June								●	●	●		
Cucumber (frame)	—	—	Apr/May	—	June							●	●	●	●	●	
Cucumber (ridge)	—	—	Apr/May	—	June								●	●	●		
Kale	Apr/May	—	—	—	Jun/Jul	●	●	●	●	●						●	●
Kohl-rabi	Mar/Aug	—	—	As reqd	—						●	●	●	●	●	●	●
Leek	Mar/Apr	—	—	—	May/Jun	●	●	●	●						●	●	●
Lettuce	Mar/Sep	—	—	As reqd	—						●	●	●	●	●		
Marrow	—	—	Apr/May	—	June								●	●	●		
Melon	—	—	May	—	June								●	●			
Mustard and Cress	All Year	—	—	—	—	●	●	●	●	●	●	●	●	●	●	●	●
Okra	May	Late Apr	—	June	—									●	●	●	
Onion (spring)	Aug–Spring	—	—	—	—	●	●	●	●	●	●	●					
Onion (Japanese)	Aug	—	—	Mar	—	○	○	○	○	○	●	●	●	○	○	○	○
Onion (bulb)	Aug–Spring	—	—	April	—	○	○	○	○	○	○	●	●	●	○	○	○
Onion (sets)	—	—	—	—	Mar/Apr	○	○	○	○	○	○	●	●	●	○	○	○
Parsnip	Feb/Mar	—	—	May	—	○	○	○	○	○	○	○				●	●
Peas (round)	Oct/Mar	—	—	—	—						●	●					
Peas (wrinkled)	Apr/Jun	—	—	—	—							●	●	●			
Peppers	—	—	April	—	June								●	●	●		
Potatoes	—	—	—	—	Mar/Apr	○	○	○	○	○	○	●	●	●	●	○	○
Pumpkin	—	—	Apr/May	June	June									●	●		
Radish	Mar/Aug	—	—	—	—						●	●	●	●	●		
Rhubarb	March	—	—	—	—		●	●	●	●	●	●					
Shallots	—	—	—	—	Jan/Mar	○	○	○	○	○	○	○	●	●	○	○	○
Spinach (summer)	Feb/May	—	—	As reqd	—						●	●	●	●	●		
Spinach (winter)	Jul/Sep	—	—	As reqd	—	●	●	●	●							●	●
Spinach (perpetual)	Apr/Jul	—	—	As reqd	—	●	●	●	●	●			●	●	●	●	●
Swede	May	—	—	June	—	○	○	○	○					●	●	●	○
Sweet Corn	—	—	Apr/May	June	May								●	●			
Tomato	—	—	Apr	—	June								●	●	●		
Turnip (roots)	Apr/Aug	—	—	As reqd	—	○	○	○	○		●	●	●	●	●	○	○
Turnip (leaves)	Sept	—	—	—	—											●	●

Key ▦ Perennials ●●●● Harvesting
  ▦ Root Crops ▦ Other Crops ○○○○ Storing

Protected Cropping

If wind blows continually through plants it will cool the leaves and slow down the speed of plant growth and development. The full effects of this are well illustrated by the stunted trees and shrubs that grow on exposed hillsides and moorlands. Hedges, fences and screens positioned in and around suburban gardens naturally 'break' the wind and the term 'sheltered' usually refers to adequate wind protection.

Almost any kind of material can be used to equal effect as a windbreak, although the wind-filtering effect of trees, shrubs and hedges is much better than a nearly impenetrable fence. The important thing to remember when erecting or planning a windbreak is that something which offers a 50 per cent obstruction to wind will be the most effective. If you build a solid wall, the wind will hit it hard, rising up the structure only to plunge over it into the vacuum formed behind. A general guide is that a shelter one unit high will give seven units length of wind protection beyond.

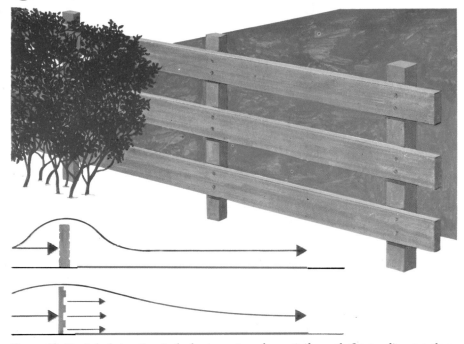

Figure 42: Partial obstruction is the best way to reduce wind speed. Centre diagram shows how an impenetrable screen can increase wind force in the lee.

Windbreak Structures

Placing twiggy sticks around early crops such as peas will give some wind protection, as will wire netting seedling guards. If you add a covering to the windbreak which lets in light and retains heat, the speed of plant growth will be increased even further. This leads on to a wide range of structures which can be used for crop protection – from low cloches, to somewhat larger frames, to – largest of all – walk-in greenhouses.

Covering Material

There are three main choices of covering material for protected cropping. Glass is at present the cheapest permanent material which will retain the maximum amount of heat and give the best light penetration. Semi-rigid, clear plastics are rapidly coming to the fore and although they are more expensive, they have obvious advantages in domestic situations, in avoiding the possibility of broken glass.

Thin polythene sheet is the cheapest material and is very useful for both suburban and commercial crop protection. Its only drawback is that its heat retention quality is not as good as that of the other materials. If you are going to use it for garden crop protection make sure you buy ultra-violet light-inhibited polythene sheet. This is usually sold as UVI polythene, and even the thinnest gauges will give enough use for one full summer and two winters. If you roll up the polythene and put it away in summer, so it is not exposed to strong ultraviolet summer sunlight, its useful life will be extended considerably. Thicker sheets used for covering greenhouse structures will have proportionally longer life, for example, the 500 gauge (125 micron) thickness will be cheaper but not as long lasting in sunlight as the proportionally more expensive 600 gauge material.

Light Reflection

Another point worth consideration is that white, silver and light colours reflect light, whilst black and dark colours absorb heat. Thus the wall of a lean-to greenhouse painted white will reflect light needed by plants and a mulch of black peat around crops under cloches will help the soil to absorb more heat. Maximum light transmission and heat retention during cold periods will give the fastest and strongest plant growth.

Materials for polythene tunnel cloche.

Hoops pushed into soil in position.

Figure 43: Cross-section across tunnel showing plants in situ.

Figure 44: Push up sheet to obtain access to plants in tunnel, for watering, cultural treatment or harvesting.

POLYTHENE TUNNEL CLOCHES

In my opinion, the polythene tunnel cloche is the most useful tool in the garden after a spade. It is cheap to buy, completely flexible in length, width and height (the wider any hoop is spaced the lower will be the coverage), easy to handle and perfectly safe. It protects crops from birds; it will bring harvesting times forward by a week or two; it keeps crops such as lettuce clean from soil splashed by rain and it is easily taken up, rolled and packed away. Irrigation presents no problems as rain running over the sides goes straight into the soil and will spread sufficiently for plant roots to take it up in all but the hottest, driest weather. When these conditions prevail, it is easy enough to raise one side of the polythene and water the plants.

There is a knack to erecting these tunnels and you are well advised to try to perfect it. The first requirements are a wire hoop with two loops, about 4 in. (10 cm) from each end of the wire and a sheet of polythene. Push hoops into the soil 3–4 ft (90–120 cm) apart. Secure one end by burying it in the soil (see right, 1 and 2). Unroll polythene over hoops and secure other end (see 3 and 4). Tension polythene by fixing a wire or rotproof string to the loop on one side, taking it over the polythene and securing it to the loop on the other side (see 5).

When you want to get at the crop for hoeing, watering and harvesting just lift one side of the sheet like a curtain, between the hoop and the tensioning wire (see right, 6). Replace it when you have finished your work.

1. Secure end either by tying or 2. by burying in soil. 3. Unroll polythene over the wires. 4. Secure other end. 5. Tension polythene with string or wire. 6. Lift sheet for access.

CLOCHES AND FRAMES

On a very small scale and for virtually no cost, small 'cloches' can be made from salvaged clear plastic containers. Just cut away the base and cover single or small groups of plants, such as radish, making sure you 'screw' the cut edge into the soil for ½ in. (1 cm) or so to prevent the wind blowing the container away. Remove the cap on the top to ventilate in very hot weather and to apply water. Lettuce grows particularly well under these containers.

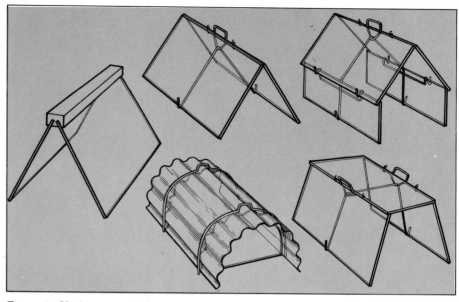

Figure 4/: Various types of cloche; from l. to r. top: home-made, tent, barn, 'Novalux' plastic sheet, flat-topped cloche.

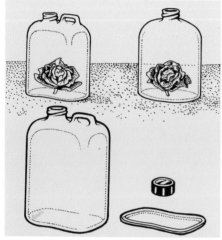

Figure 45: Clear plastic containers can be turned into 'cloches'.

On a similar principle, old glass jars placed over such seedlings as marrow and ridge cucumber during the early raising stages will provide favourable conditions for germination and growth of these vegetables.

There is a variety of glass and plastic cloches which can be used singly or placed end to end to construct a continuous row. Rainfall on all these cloches will run down the sides and into the soil to the crop, so special watering arrangements are not necessary. The simplest glass cloche of all is made by clipping two sheets together and there are several proprietary clips sold for this purpose. You could even make your own by sawing two cuts in a cube of wood and fitting them over the glass (see figure 47).

'Do-it-Yourself' Covers

Another simple glass cover can be constructed using a wooden box, merely by removing the base and placing a sheet of glass on top of it (see figure 46). Step up the dimensions of this and you have a cold frame, for the basis of a frame is just four side walls with a sloping glass or clear plastic covered roof. A single frame has one taller side at the back and a double frame is just higher at the centre (see figure 46).

The clear roof of these frames comprises several wooden or metal framed units to hold the glass or plastic, known as 'frames' or 'lights'. In hot weather you should raise the lights fractionally to provide ventilation, but keep them closed at night and in cold weather. You can use these frames to raise seeds and propagate cuttings, as well as for growing crops such as cucumbers, lettuce and melons to maturity.

Very keen gardeners may also heat their frame. There are three methods of heating: electrical soil-warming cables (probably the best way to heat frames); an electric tube heater fitted to one frame wall; or the cheapest method of all, placing the frame on top of a bed of fresh manure (known as a 'hot bed') covered with soil. Heat is generated from the decomposing manure and speeds plant growth accordingly. Hot beds can be used effectively for such crops as early carrots, but they are especially good for cucumbers and melons.

GLASSHOUSES

Glasshouses may have a basic structure of wood or metal; wood, especially red cedar, will last well, but aluminium structures are undoubtedly the best. They require no maintenance and offer the very least obstruction to light. Modern designs can be

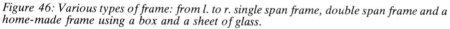

Figure 46: Various types of frame: from l. to r. single span frame, double span frame and a home-made frame using a box and a sheet of glass.

purchased packed in cases to be taken home and erected easily over a weekend or so.

If the glasshouse is artificially heated the range of crops you can grow, especially in autumn, winter and spring, is increased yet again. The cost of heating may however be the deciding factor, and in cold, exposed conditions more heat – incurring greater cost – will be needed. Hedges and screens around the glasshouse will break the wind and, as long as they are far enough away to avoid casting shadows across the house, will also save heat. Bear in mind that the cost of heating is likely to be twice as much on a windy day as on a calm one.

There are a few other factors to remember about heating and heat loss. One is that the greater the surface area of the structure, the greater the heat loss will be. Long narrow houses have a greater surface area than an almost square one. If you raise the side walls of a glasshouse, for example, on the traditionally shaped house 6 ft × 4 ft (180 × 120 cm) from 4 ft (120 cm) to 6 ft (180 cm), you increase the surface area through which heat can be lost by 40 sq ft (3·7 sq m). Compare this kind of house with the total surface area of the 10 ft × 12 ft (3 m × 4 m) polythene tunnel house (see overleaf) which has some 300 sq ft (27 sq m). The polythene house will have about 2½ sq ft (0·2 sq m) of outer structure for every 1 sq ft (900 sq cm) of covered soil, while the tall 6 ft × 4 ft (180 × 120 cm) house will have 7½ sq ft

Figure 48: Three examples of glasshouse; from l. to r. lean-to, traditionally shaped brick-based and glasshouse made of Dutch Light.

(0·7 sq m) to 1 sq ft (900 sq cm) covered. Houses less than 8 ft × 8 ft (240 × 240 cm) are really too small in practice to heat easily and ventilate adequately.

Heat Loss

Heat is lost more rapidly through polythene than glass but the polythene structure is virtually air tight, while heat will be lost through the gaps between panes with glass.

Finally, the greater the temperature difference between inside and outside,

the greater will be the heat loss. It is much cheaper to keep a house just frost free through the winter than it is to hold a near tropical temperature inside when conditions are near arctic outside. You can reduce heat loss in such conditions by erecting a sheet of polythene on the north side of the house to give the effect of double glazing. If you line the whole house you will have a 35 per cent loss of light which is too great; lining the north side only gives an acceptable 18 per cent loss of light.

The rule-of-thumb method of calculating the amount of heat needed is to begin by measuring the surface area of the house. To keep the house at a chosen temperature evenly each square foot of surface area needs 1·4 BTUs (British Thermal Units) per hour for every degree Fahrenheit of difference between the outside temperature and your chosen heat level. If, for example, you wish to hold an 8 × 8 ft (2·4 × 2·4 m) greenhouse, which will have 64 square feet (5·76 sq m) of surface area, at 40°F (4·4°C) through the winter and the temperature outdoors might drop to 20°F (−5·4°C) your heater would need to be able to produce 7000 to 8000 BTUs an hour.

Electric heaters and natural gas and high-grade paraffin burners may be used to provide heat. Paraffin and natural gas burners tend to release moisture and if the atmosphere becomes to damp it may be necessary to ventilate the house slightly.

Figure 49: A sheet of polythene lining against the north side of a glasshouse, and nearby hedges forming screens, reduce heat loss in winter.

N

POLYTHENE TUNNEL GREENHOUSE

By stepping up the size of cloches and frames even further, you can progress to the walk-in structures, more commonly known as greenhouses. These again can be of glass or polythene – a polythene-clad house being cheaper than a glasshouse as it is a lighter structure and cheaper materials can be used in its construction.

Although it perhaps takes a fairly enthusiastic gardener to construct and manage one, a greenhouse does considerably extend the range of crops that can be grown. For most people the provision of heavy tomato crops alone is sufficient incentive! Building a polythene tunnel house is very well within the do-it-yourself operator's capability and I recommend variations on the basic Lee Valley Experimental Horticulture Station designs, which have been developed mainly for commercial growers. In fact these are useful not only for gardening, but also for covering such things as sand-pits and similar outdoor play areas for children.

The following instructions are for the construction of a polythene-covered house, which would completely cover the 10 ft × 12 ft (3 m × 4 m) plot. If, however, you reduced the height – the width and the area of soil covered would be correspondingly increased.

You will need:

3 × 21 ft (6·4 m) lengths ½ in (1 cm) bore galvanised water pipe (hoops)

2 ×5 ft (1·5 m) lengths ½ in (1 cm)

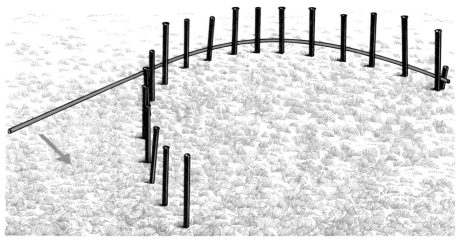

Figure 50: End posts must be secure before bending the pipe.

A metal sheet around the posts helps achieve a circular bend.

One person can easily construct the framework of the house alone.

bore galvanised pipe (ridge pieces)

6 × 2 ft (60 cm) lengths 1 in (2·5 m) bore galvanised pipe (foundation stakes)

1 × 20 ft (6 m) length of 10 gauge galvanised fencing wire

4 × 8 ft (2·4 m) lengths of 2 in × 2 in (5 × 5 cm) timber (lintels for doors)

2 × 4 ft (1·2 m) lengths of 2 in × 2 in (5 × 5 cm) timber (lintels for doors)

4 × 6 ft (1·8 m) lengths of 2 in × 1 in (5 × 2·5 m) timber★

2 × 4 ft (1·2 m) lengths of 2 in × 1 in (5 × 2·5 cm) timber★

Quantity of laths for roller blind door

Quantity of nails

1 sheet polythene film 24 ft × 24 ft (7·3 ×7·3 m) 500 gauge (125 micron) (be sure it is *Ultraviolet Inhibited* (sold as UVI) film))

★Any thin lath wood; alternatively staples and wire will do for this.

Construction

Drive a series of short posts into the ground and bend the three 21 ft lengths (6·4 m) of pipe round them to form a semi-circular hoop 12 ft (4 m) in diameter. Then measure the site to mark out a 10 ft × 12 ft (3 m × 4 m) area. Take out a trench 10 in (25 cm) wide and 12 in (30 cm) deep around the outside, 2 in (5 cm) out from the marked plot. Throw the soil out of the area, *not* into it. Drive the 2 ft (60 cm)

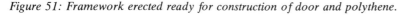

Figure 51: Framework erected ready for construction of door and polythene.

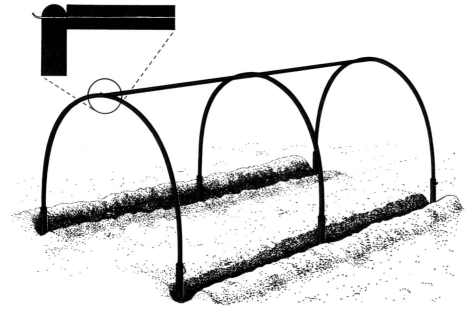

36

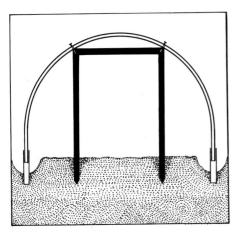

Figure 52: Door frame in position.

Long nails are used to hold door blind.

(1·2 m) cross timbers in place by driving nails through holes in the hoops, through the cross pieces and into the uprights. (Alternatively use thick strips of rubber over the pipes and nail them to the cross pieces and uprights.)

Cover all rough or sharp edges with insulating tape or strips of polythene, and then cover the whole structure with the polythene sheet.

Covering

This must fit firmly to give the whole structure strength and wind resistance. If it is allowed to flap it will quickly wear through. Fit the cover in warm weather because as the film cools it will shrink and tighten further.

Cover the frame with the sheet, making sure the 'skirt' around the base is the same length all the way round. Fill in trenches with soil – firming it so as to tighten the film over the frame.

Cut out the polythene inside the lintels, fold the polythene edge around the lintels and nail it securely with timber laths and nails. Make the doors either as lift-up blinds or as polythene-covered frames secured as sliding doors. (Both doors must be open to ventilate the structure adequately.)

long foundation stakes firmly into the ground, one at each corner and one in the centre of each side. Leave 6–9 in (15–23 cm) protruding above ground.

Drill a hole through the foundation stakes and the end of each hoop and place the hoops in the foundation stakes to erect the main structure. Secure by putting a short piece of wire or bolt through both holes you have drilled. If the polythene cover becomes slack at any future time, you can lift up the hoop a fraction, drill another hole and secure in the same

way to take up the slack.

Drill a hole horizontally through the top of each hoop, making sure it is in the top and centre. Thread wire through the hole in an end hoop, through the length of one ridge piece, through the centre hoop, through the next ridge pipe and through the other end hoop. Secure both ends of the wire to form a rigid structure.

Bury the base of the 8 ft (2·4 m) long 2 × 2 in (5 × 5 cm) wooden uprights 4 ft (1·2 m) apart into the soil to construct the door lintels. Hold the 4 ft

Figure 53: The polythene house completed. Note that it has doors at either end for through ventilation.

Irrigation Principles

The evaporation of moisture from a plant's leaves gives it energy to suck in more water and plant foods through its roots. While this may be an over-simplification of the complete process, for simple vegetable growing it is a sufficient interpretation. The strength and amount of sunlight, the temperature, the humidity of the surrounding atmosphere and the effect of drying winds all control the speed of plant growth. If the drying effects are greater than the moisture available to be taken up by the roots, leaves will begin to wilt. Wilting prevents too great a loss of moisture in plants.

Although initial wilting provides protection for the plant, it also slows down growth. This means less rapidly produced succulent tissue, while any growth that does occur is likely to be unpalatable, tough, stringy and fibrous. If you want succulent vegetables, therefore, it is worth ensuring that most of your plants, do not lack water. I say most because there are some exceptions to this general rule – turnips that grow rapidly will be succulent and possess the desired mild flavour, but if, for example, tomatoes have too much lush growth, the fruits are likely to be watery, pale coloured and have a poor flavour.

Moderation applies as much to watering as any other garden practice and you should aim to avoid both water-logged and desert-dry soils. As I have stressed before, the addition of plenty of well-rotted organic matter, manure, compost and similar materials is a great help in controlling the amount of water in soil. It improves drainage in waterlogged soils, and helps light, sandy soils to retain water.

When supplies are short, use water already used for washing up, bathing or washing clothes, unless bleach or bath salts have been added.

'Lay Flat' polythene tubing being used to irrigate seedlings.

Drainage

Digging ditches and constructing pipe and clinker drains to drain water-logged soil is not very practical for most gardens. Where, for example, do you drain off water, if you have neighbours on three sides? If your garden tends to be waterlogged (usually a problem in winter and spring) the most efficient way to drain it is probable to build up the level of your small vegetable plot. The water will then drain from the plot into the gulleys, paths, lawns and other surrounding areas. You will actually raise the plot automatically by adding organic matter and repeatedly digging the soil. Next time you have the opportunity, look at one of those very well culti-vated country cottage gardens, and you will invariably see that the level of the cultivated area is above the path.

Waterlogged plots can be improved, then, by raising the level, which you can do by digging in plenty of organic matter and also by adding coarse sand and well-weathered ashes in modera-tion. Light, sandy soils, however, have an opposing problem: they dry out too quickly. Here the solution lies in adding organic matter to hold water thereby stopping it from just draining away. If you 'mulch' the surface of the soil which means covering it with peat, well-rotted compost and leaves, the speed at which water evaporates from the surface will also be reduced.

Evaporation

Water evaporates from wet soil at much the same rate as it does from soil which is maintaining a crop of vegetables. On a bright summer's day something like 2–3 mm of water will be lost and 20–30 mm of rain (25 mm = 1 in) would be needed after eight to ten

Figure 54: 'Lay Flat' polythene tubing is one of the simplest and most efficient forms of irrigation.

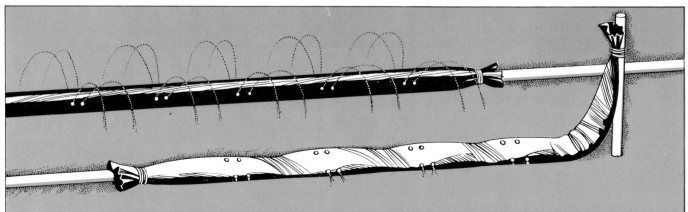

bright days to make up the evaporation. Strong-growing weeds will drain the soil of water to the same extent as vegetables, which is one of the reasons why it is important to control weeds. If the surface of the soil is dry and especially if it is hoed to maintain a shallow layer of fine dry soil or 'tilth', it will lose very little water.

Once soil gets really dry it is virtually impossible to *partially* moisten it throughout. The immediate remedy is to saturate the surface, after which the more water you add the greater will be the depth of saturation. This is why it is better to water really well occasionally than give repeated light waterings which will do little more than just dampen the surface. The surface, after all, is actually the place where it is important to retain a dry tilth which will then preserve moisture at a lower level.

Watering Equipment

There is an amazing range of automatic and semi-automatic watering or irrigating equipment on the market – from static spray nozzles to automatically oscillating sprinklers. Most of these, in my opinion, are rather expensive luxuries and there are really only three pieces of equipment that you need. In order of priority these are a good watering can, a hose long enough to reach the vegetable plot and 'Lay-Flat' polythene irrigation tube.

Bear in mind that watering from the spout of a can or the end of a hose produces very heavy water droplets and applications of this kind, unless carefully applied, can batter down the soil surface, destroying the tilth you are trying to retain. The closer the spout is to the soil and therefore the more gentle the delivery, the better. As long as it is delivered carefully, however, water directed to one area does penetrate better than if you spread a small amount of water over a larger surface. This is just quickly lost in evaporation.

If you need to repeatedly water single plants such as tomatoes, a good tip is to sink a flower pot into the soil close to the plant. Keep this repeatedly filled with water, which will then trickle slowly through the base of the pot getting moisture down to the area of roots where it is required. It also prevents pressure of water applied in other ways from destroying the soil structure.

It is difficult to find out just how much water is required by plants

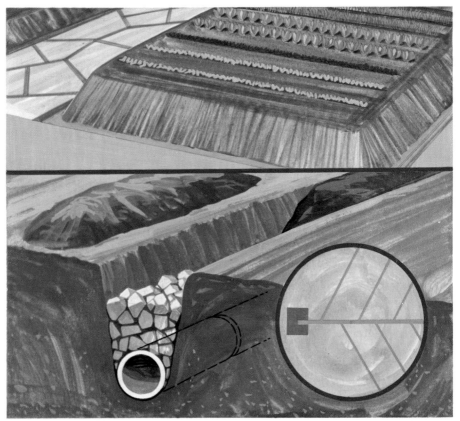

Figure 55: Two ways of effecting soil drainage. Top, by raising the level of the plot with repeated digging and adding organic matter. Bottom, in extreme cases, by constructing pipe and clinker drains. The inset shows the pattern for laying drains, the small square being a 'sump' made from a bin punctured at the bottom and filled with rubble, sunk below ground level.

without getting a spade or trowel and actually digging to see the dampness of the soil 6–8 in (15–20 cm) down. As a guide, if the soil looks and feels damp when you dig down all will be well, but if it does not, a really good watering will be necessary to get the required penetration. Whatever you do, avoid deep digging during drying

Figure 56: A good way to water plants that need constant irrigation.

and drought conditions as this will speed evaporation considerably.

By far the best method of watering vegetables and many other plants is through 'Lay-Flat' black polythene tube which has tiny holes punctured in it at 6, 12 or 18 in (15, 30 or 45 cm) intervals. 'Lay-flat' describes the way the tube is packed and the black polythene prevents green algae growth inside the tube. To use it unroll the tube along the rows and place it close to the stems of plants. Then use any pressure source (from the mains or a syphon from a rainwater tank) to feed water into the tube. It will slowly drip through the holes into the soil and, if left running for long enough, the steady, gentle flow will give deep penetration. If you increase the water pressure or reduce the length of tube, the water will spurt from the holes in small jets rather than drip so increasing the watered area. Low water pressure and steady dripping gives the most efficient water distribution.

Fertilisers can be added at the same time as watering – liquid kinds when watering with a can, and powdered fertilisers under the trickle tube connected to a hose.

Growing Your Own Vegetables

It is difficult to over-emphasise just how easy it is to grow almost all kinds of vegetable. Yet, understandably, when faced with yields perhaps not quite as good as hoped for, or when starting out with a new plot, many gardeners may feel that the brief instructions available on seed packets are not sufficiently informative to ensure really first-class produce. For this reason, we have given here complete cultural and harvesting details for each individual vegetable, covering the whole cycle from siting, sowing and growing to harvesting.

The wide range of different varieties of vegetable now available to home-growers has added a great deal to the experimental interest and fun of vegetable-growing, so as much coverage as space permits has been included for some of the less familiar types. Try to find a good retailer in your locality who is interested in vegetables and ready to help you in your selection. He should have up-to-the-minute information on new varieties, for which there are often claims of earlier and heavier yields, better quality and higher resistance to pest and disease. But grow new varieties alongside old faithfuls rather than always going for novelty, so that you can gradually assess what best suits your garden conditions, as well as your palate.

Of course, no one has perfect site and soil conditions for growing every kind of vegetable, although repeated cultivation and the addition of organic matter will do much to improve them. Crops such as potatoes and peas will also help, in breaking-in soil not previously or recently used for vegetables and our information in the section that follows should help you to select crops that are likely to give satisfactory yields in the conditions provided by your own plot.

When sowing seed, try to avoid the temptation to sow it too thickly and deeply. Most seeds need no more than a light covering of soil, particularly if the soil is good and moist. In dry conditions, it is worth running some water along the base of the drill before sowing, especially if you are using pelleted seed. Germination depends to some extent on weather conditions and the vegetable in question, but in most cases, it takes two or three weeks – longer in cold weather.

It is hard to give hard and fast rulings on how many vegetables a packet of seed or a certain length of row will produce. Again, this can be subject to the vagaries of soil and weather. Wherever possible, we have attempted to give an indication of average yields, but remember that a heavier crop of such vegetables as tomato and sweet corn can be expected after a warm, sunny summer than after a cool, damp one. For root and leafy crops, such as carrots and cabbages, the reverse is true.

Pests and other problems affecting vegetables are discussed briefly in each case, but further information on dealing with them, should you need it, is given on pages 112 to 115. The 'tips' are snippets of useful information gained from my personal experience of vegetable-growing.

Artichokes

Apart from sharing a name and the fact that they are both perennial vegetables the Globe and Jerusalem artichokes have little in common and are really best considered separately.

GLOBE ARTICHOKE

The large 'globe' shaped flower buds produced by these plants (*Cynara scolymus*) should be cut green to provide a delectable vegetable. They are cooked by boiling in salted water for ½–¾ hour and may be eaten hot or served cold with a vinaigrette sauce. One large globe will provide an adequate serving for two people. The plant produces very attractively cut silvery-grey leaves.

Site and Soil

Choose a sheltered sunny site in a fenced or hedged-round garden. Dig the soil well and improve it by adding well-rotted compost and/or manure. This gives strong growth and increases the number of 'globes'. Avoid planting in heavy wet soils.

Special Siting

One to three plants should be sufficient for the average small garden. Three could certainly be planted to the northerly or westerly side of a 10 ft × 12 ft (3 × 4 m) vegetable plot. The bold leaves provide shelter for smaller plants, but will not cast shade if planted on the north and west side.

Propagating and Planting

Either buy young suckers (the side shoots growing around the main stem) or cut from established plants in April (see figure 57). Plant out suckers in the cropping site 2–2½ ft (60–75 cm) apart (see figure 57). If the soil is very fertile, go for the wider spacing. Firm the suckers well. The cut root stem will soon produce roots and grow away to provide flower buds which you can cut in August and September. The best

Globe Artichokes. *Figure 57: (Below) Propagating Globe Artichokes from suckers.*

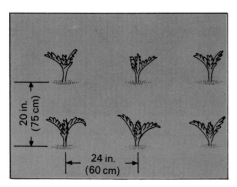

crops occur in the second and third year – after this, plant out more suckers to replace three-year old plants. Old plants yield smaller and fewer buds.

Give the newly planted offsets plenty of water in dry weather until they are well established. Hoe occasionally to eliminate weeds. In early winter, when the leaves start to die down, cut away the old flower stems and tie the younger leaves up together before drawing soil up round the stems. This soil will help protect the tender crowns from frost damage.

Harvesting

You can start cropping established plants in July, when the flower buds are plump and fully swollen and before the scales have hard brown tips. Cut them with secateurs, taking the large central, or 'king' globe, first and subsequently harvesting the smaller side-shoot globes. Once the scales turn purplish and the flowers begin to show, the buds are inedible.

Possible Problems

Lack of moisture and poor soil give small, hard and woody globes. Try watering the plants with foliar fertiliser to give a quick improvement. Subsequently add general fertiliser in spring at the rate of 2–3 oz per sq yd (60–85 gms per sq m) and mulch with well-rotted manure or compost to improve plant growth.

Jerusalem Artichokes.

Figure 58: Jerusalem Artichokes form an attractive screen.

> ### USEFUL TIP
> A single plant or group of two or three look very attractive in a herbaceous border and to the front of a shrub border. Remember they grow 3–4 ft (90–120 cm) high.

JERUSALEM ARTICHOKE

This plant (*Helianthus tuberosus*) is grown for the tubers which are like

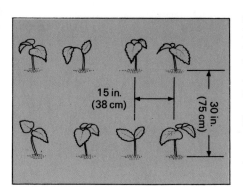

knobbly potatoes. The stems grow 6–8 ft (1·8–2·5 m) high and are perfect for a quick summer screen, perhaps to hide an ugly shed or form a temporary hedge in a new garden (see figure 58). The soft green sunflower leaves are also useful as a background foil to flower arrangements but remember that cutting the foliage will inevitably reduce the vegetable crop.

Site and Soil

Full sun or sun and partial shade provide suitable sites. Any soil, even the worst possible, will provide tubers, although better soils produce heavier crops.

Propagating and Planting

Save a few small tubers from your previous crop or purchase a few to start your cropping from scratch. Plant the tubers in spring, from February onwards, 3–6 in (7·5–15 cm) deep, 15 in (38 cm) apart.

How to Grow

Hoe to eliminate weeds, cut down foliage in autumn and pinch out tips to prevent flower buds developing.

Harvesting

The tubers will be ready for harvesting in late autumn. Either leave them in the soil and dig them up as you want them, or lift and store them in a shed.

Possible Problems

Lift tubers in the autumn if slugs start to eat holes in them.

> ### USEFUL TIP
> The variety 'Fuseau' has a very good flavour and a smooth skin which makes it much easier to peel.

Asparagus

Commercial asparagus (*Asparagus officinalis*) crops are cut by hand and the high wage costs go to make the delicious tasting asparagus spears almost prohibitively expensive! Once established in your garden, however, asparagus will crop year after year with very little trouble and at virtually no cost. The feathery green foliage, sometimes called 'grass' or 'fern', is also used in floral decorations, but cut sparingly if you want a good crop of spears the following year.

Site and Soil

Select an open sunny site and well drained soil. Light soils tending to be sandy are ideal; add sand to very heavy soils to improve drainage. Dig the soil very thoroughly in the autumn to remove all perennial weed roots, and add as much well-rotted garden compost and manure as you can get. Once planted, the crop can stay down for twenty years, so it is wise to see it has a good foundation free of perennial weeds.

Sowing and Propagating

Sow seed 2 in (5 cm) deep in the open soil in April to raise new plants, and thin the seedlings to stand 6 in (15 cm) apart when they are big enough to handle. Always use fresh seed – if it is more than one year old it quickly loses its germination properties, (see Seed Germination chart, page 18).

A more common way of starting asparagus is to buy one- or two-year-old seedlings (called one-year and two-year 'Asparagus Crowns') in April. This saves a full year's growing time. Don't let these crowns get dry – if you have to delay planting them for a few days store in damp peat.

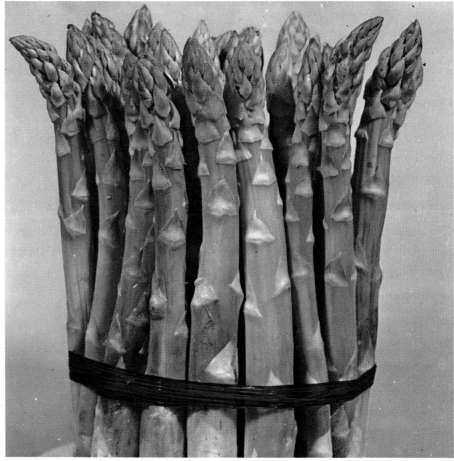

A bunch of Asparagus spears.

How to Grow

Dig out a trench 8–10 in (20–25 cm) deep and 12 in (30 cm) wide. Then form a shallow ridge 3 in (7·5 cm) high at the base (see figure 59). Space the crowns 15–18 in (38–45 cm) apart with the string-like roots spread over both sides of the ridge. Then cover them with 2–3 in (5–7·5 cm) of soil and subsequently, when hoeing to control weeds, slowly fill up the trench with soil. Space the rows 4–5 ft (120–150 cm) apart if you are growing more than one row.

When the foliage is fully grown you may have to erect a few stakes and run a string or wire down each side of the row to support the stems and prevent them blowing over. Cut the foliage down to within 2 in (5 cm) of the soil in the autumn. In fact the time to do this is usually just after the first frost when

Figure 59: Planting a single row of Asparagus crowns.

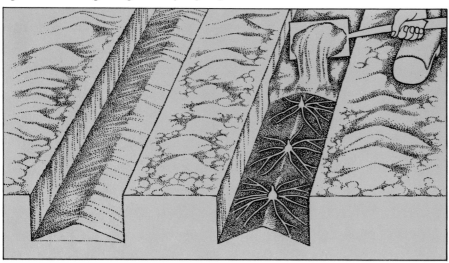

Asparagus spears at harvest time.

the foliage turns yellow and before the berries on female plants fall to the ground. If the berries are allowed to fall they will produce scattered seedlings which will be difficult to remove from the established cropping crowns. Cutting the foliage too early reduces the build-up of vigour in the crowns for the next season's crop.

Each autumn and spring, earth up the rows by drawing 1–2 in (2·5–5 cm) of soil each side of the row. The greater the depth of soil covering the crowns, the longer will be the blanched stem. If you prefer more green stem, then less earthing up is necessary.

Sprinkle general fertiliser along the row in spring at the rate of 2–3 oz per sq yd (60–85 gms per sq m). Mulch with well-rotted compost after mid-June to smother seedling weeds, retain moisture and improve both the soil and asparagus growth in future years.

Figure 61: Support growing foliage with stakes and wires to keep tidy rather than cutting it back which reduces the ensuing crop.

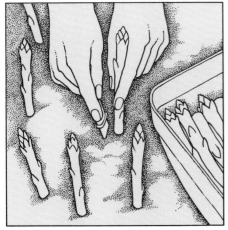

Figure 60: Cutting Asparagus spears.

Harvesting
A year after planting out, one spear can be cut from each crown. The following year all the spears can·be cut over a 4-week period and in the third year (when plants are four to five years old) spears can be cut for six weeks. Stop *all* cutting by mid-June to allow the plants to build up strength for the next season's crop.

Cut the spears (i.e. the emerging shoots) when they are 4–6 in (10–15 cm) above the soil. Always cut them before the tip starts to open into foliage producing shoots. This means cutting spears every three days or so in cooler weather and almost daily in hot weather. An old kitchen knife with a broken end is the perfect cutting tool. Sharpen the squared-off end, run this gently down the side of the spear and cut approximately 2–4 in (5–10 cm) below the soil surface. After practice it is also possible to bend the shoots towards you and snap the spears from the crowns by hand.

Asparagus foliage in summer.

Possible Problems
If you see the foliage and young growth being eaten by greyish grubs and their parent asparagus beetles, dust or spray with Derris. After cutting, BHC dust and sprays could be used.

Note
Asparagus is a perennial and not a rotational crop, which makes it unsuitable for inclusion in the 10 ft × 12 ft (3 m × 4 m) vegetable plot. Ideally, find a spot elsewhere in the garden for the vegetable.

USEFUL TIP

Be sure to cut regularly, ideally every day, to get the most palatable spears. If you are not going to cook at once stand the cut ends in cool water for a while before standing in a cool place. If you leave the spears too long, they will go stale, limp and slightly bitter.

Aubergines

Commonly called 'Egg Plant', presumably because of the plump egg-like shape, the fruits of aubergine plants (*Solanum melongena ovigerum*) have a subtle flavour which is popular in America and becoming increasingly so in Britain.

Aubergine plants need growing conditions similar to those for tomatoes and if anything you will find them easier to grow than the tomato, although possibly not quite so easy as the third *Solanum*, potato. All three plants have the typical *Solanum* flowers, but the purple and yellow of the aubergines are the largest and most attractive.

Site and Soil

If you are not growing the plants in a greenhouse or polythene covered structure or frame, choose a warm, sunny and sheltered site, such as a south-facing fence or wall. On heavy soils, which are low and tend to stay wet, raise small hills of soil to give better drainage to the planting position. Best results will be achieved in either light soils containing plenty of well-rotted organic matter or in pots and bags filled with proprietary growing composts.

Sowing Instructions

Sow seed in a temperature of 55°–60°F (13°–15°C) – the earlier in spring this can be done the longer the cropping period and the heavier the crop. Where night temperatures of below 50°F (10°C) occur, delay sowing rather than risk the chance of a check to the growth of young plants, which will die if subjected to frost. You can sow in pots in late March and stand these on the window sill indoors. Transplant to

Figure 62: Aubergines grow well in fertilised peat bags.

Figure 63: Pinch out growing tips.

Aubergines growing on the plant.

larger pots to go on a patio or balcony in June. These plants will yield fruit in late summer and early autumn.

A warmer climate and a long growing period will give you crops of ten to twelve fruits, each one weighing up to 1 lb (450 gms). A shorter growing season gives four to six fruits per plant.

How to Grow

After germination move the seedlings to a 3½ in (9 cm) diameter pot. As they grow too large for this, either plant out in the cropping position or put into a much larger pot, 6–7 ins (15–17.5 cm) diameter. When the plants are 6 ins (15 cm) high, pinch out the growing tip to encourage several branches to form (see figure 63). Reduce the number of young branches once the required number of fruits start to swell. This will avoid too many very

small fruits being produced. Give plenty of water in dry weather and a liquid feed (tomato food is ideal) every ten to fourteen days once the fruits start to swell.

Harvesting

When the fruits have a rich purple shine (in late summer/early autumn) they are ready to gather. Cut them with secateurs or a sharp knife to avoid bruising. Once the fruit lose their shine they also lose their flavour.

Possible Problems

In hot dry conditions, especially under glass and polythene, the tiny insect – Red Spider Mite – turns the leaves a yellow/bronze colour. Syringe with water to deter this pest (this will also help the flowers to set fruit). Control severe attacks with products based on azobenzene and malathion.

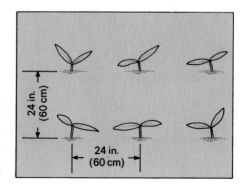

Beans

Broad Beans (*Vicia faba*) are one of the easiest of all vegetables to grow, and cooked with bacon when they are young and tender, they are a real delicacy. Some people say the pods can be eaten if gathered very young, but it is more usual to shell these beans before cooking. A close relative of the Broad Bean is grown by farmers for high protein cattle feed and the fragrance of these fields in flower in late spring and early summer is memorable. Broad Beans also have this fragrance when they are in flower.

Varieties

There are two main types available from seed merchants – 'White Seeded' and 'Green Seeded'. The green seeded are said to be better flavoured but all are delicious gathered young. These two types can be further divided into

Broad Beans.

Figure 64: If black fly appears on Broad Beans pinch out growing tips.

two groups, the 'Longpod' types which include the hardy varieties for autumn and winter sowing and the 'Windsor' type, which is not so hardy and therefore should be sown in spring. The 'Windsor' varieties have only about four beans per pod compared with six to nine beans yielded by the 'Longpods'. The dwarf varieties, such as 'The Midget', are particularly suitable for the small vegetable plot. The plants can be spaced 9–12 in (23–30 cm) apart in single rows and each one produces three or four stems, covered with clusters of short pods.

Site and Soil

All garden sites and soil will give reasonable results, but try to choose a site sheltered from cold winds for autumn and early spring grown crops grown without protection. Well culti-vated soils will give the heaviest yields – over 6 lb (2·7 kg) to a 10 ft (3 m) row.

Sowing Instructions

Sow beans 2 in (5 cm) deep in the open garden in late October/early November and from February to April. Space 9–12 in (23–30 cm) apart in double rows with 18 in–2 ft (45–60 cm) between them. Early sowings not only give earlier crops but often the heaviest yields as well. Try sowing some seeds indoors in pots in early February, and plant them out under cloches as soon as soil conditions allow, these will yield the earliest beans of all.

How to Grow

The stronger growing early sown Longpod types may need to be supported as they grow. If so, push a few canes into the soil either side of the beans and run a string around the row to hold up the plants. Apart from this, just hoe occasionally to control weeds.

Harvesting

Start to gather the lower pods as soon as the beans are large enough to shell out (the pods will be about ½ in (1 cm) wide). If you leave the beans to get very large and the scar, where the bean seed joins the pod, has turned brown or black, they will be too old to eat. Use such beans as next year's seed!

> **USEFUL TIP**
> Once early sown crops are gathered, cut the stems almost to the ground and water well with liquid fertiliser to get a second flush of growth and a small late crop.

Possible Problems

Black fly are often a nuisance on the growing tips in mid-summer (early sowings have usually cropped before this becomes a problem). You can control the pest on the later sown crops by pinching out the growing tips as the black fly arrive (see figure 64).

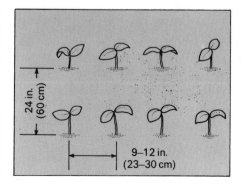

Dwarf French Beans.

DWARF FRENCH BEANS
and
HARICOT BEANS

Dwarf French Beans (*Phaseolus vulgaris*) and Haricot Beans (*Phaseolus lunatus*) are among the easiest, quickest and most prolific garden vegetables to grow and are ideal for deep freezing. There are many different varieties and it is important to select from the correct group for your own requirements. The most popular and best known to everyone from the supermarkets' deep freeze cabinets are the bush varieties. As their name indicates they grow on low bushy plants 12–28 in (30–45 cm) high, with rounded – sometimes called pencil-podded – pods 4–6 in (10–15 cm) long. The whole pod should be picked whilst young and they 'snap' easily when being prepared to cook, which is doubtless why they are sometimes called 'Snap Beans'. A smooth waxy finish to the pods in some varieties accounts for the 'Wax-Podded' type which have green and yellow pods. As well as varieties with pencil-shaped pods there are flat-podded ones which require the same cultural treatment. Less common, but especially suitable for growing under glass

Haricot Beans – yellow-podded variety.

and polythene for early crops, are the climbing varieties usually known as 'Climbing French' or 'Pole Beans'.

Finally there are those varieties which are grown for the seeds, commonly called 'Haricot', 'Butter' and 'Lima Beans'. These generally need somewhat warmer conditions to allow the beans to develop fully, after which they can be shelled out from the pods and stored. Stored beans should be soaked in water before cooking. Choose white seeded cultivars for this – dark coloured ones will be tough and inedible.

Site and Soil

An open sunny site will give the best crops and any well-cultivated garden soil is suitable. Like peas, bean roots use bacteria to fix nitrogen from the air and convert it to nitrogenous plant food. As a result they leave the soil richer in nitrogen.

Special Siting

Dwarf French Beans are the perfect window box vegetable. Try growing them also in plant tubs, patio containers and pots (see figure 66) on patios, balconies and roof gardens.

Sowing Instructions

To get the heaviest crops sow seeds to produce four plants per 1 sq ft (900 sq cm) of garden, i.e. put five plants per 12 in (16 per metre) of row and space rows 16 in (41 cm) apart. Time sowing so that when the first tender shoots poke through there is no more possibility of frost. In warm districts this will be early May – fourteen days earlier if cloche protection can be provided and fourteen days later in cold areas.

If you are sowing under glass you can either sow five to seven seeds per 7 in (17·5 cm) diameter pot, or put them direct into the border soil from

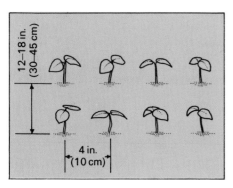

early February (or as soon as a temperature of 55°F (13°C) can be provided). Sow seeds direct where they are to grow, 1–2 in (2·5–5 cm) deep either in a drill or just push them into the soil along the row.

How to Grow

Hoe occasionally to keep down weeds and in hot dry weather water the plants well and also syringe them from overhead. In hot dry atmospheres the flowers will just drop off and fail to set

Figure 66: Dwarf Beans growing in a pot.

but you can avoid attack from this pest by keeping plants well watered. If flowers fall without forming beans, dryness is the most likely cause. Watch for slugs in spring on heavy, wet soil.

```
USEFUL TIP
Keep picking regularly and give the
plants a good watering with liquid
fertiliser after the first heavy picking
to encourage a second flush of
beans from the same plants.
```

Figure 65: Two strings support a thick row of Dwarf Beans.

pods. Support climbing french beans with canes, sticks, nets or strings as soon as they start to grow.

Harvesting

Gather all but the haricot beans when young. Test for ripeness by snapping the pod in half – if it breaks in half with a succulent 'crack' leaving no 'string' between the two halves it is ready for picking. One row along the 10 ft (3 m) length of the plot is likely to yield approximately 2–3 lb (1–1·3 kg) of fresh pods during the season.

Possible Problems

If beans are grown under glass and in hot dry atmospheres, Red Spider Mite may turn the leaves a dull, rusty, yellowish green. Syringe repeatedly with water to deter attack. If beans are grown out of doors few problems are likely.

Greenfly are sometimes a problem,

RUNNER or SCARLET RUNNER BEANS

The runner bean (*Phaseolus coccineus* syn. *Phaseolus multiflorus*) is one of Britain's most popular fresh garden vegetables, no doubt because it is tasty, prolific and very easy to grow. Commercial growers are paying more and more attention to machine harvesting french beans and this, coupled with the high cost of wages for hand picking runner beans, makes the runners comparatively more expensive to buy in the greengrocers' shops – another stimulus to home production!

Site and Soil

Runner beans will grow in partial shade, but an open sunny site is best. They will also crop in all well-dug garden soils, but the more organic matter in the form of peat, well-rotted compost and manure dug into the soil to retain moisture, the heavier will be the crop.

Sowing Instructions

Sow the large seeds 1–2 in (2–5 cm) deep, direct where they are to grow, a week or so before the likely date of your last frost in spring. This means mid-May for most areas, late April in warm districts and where cloche protection can be given, and late

Figure 67: Runner Beans grown in peat-filled bags, and (below) to form a 'wig-wam'.

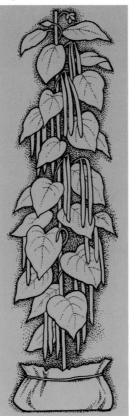

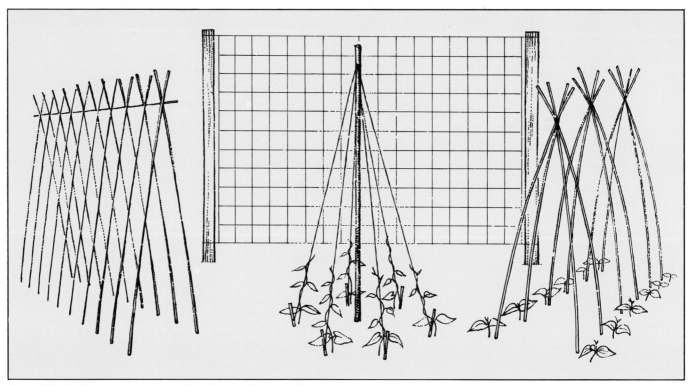

Figure 68: Various ways of supporting Runner Beans as they grow.

May/early June for cold districts. Sow enough seeds to give four plants per 3 ft (90 cm) of row, up to eight plants per sq yd (0·83 sq m) for maximum yield.

How to Grow

It is possible to grow runner beans unsupported like dwarf beans, if you pinch out the growing tips every time they exceed 12–18 in (30–45 cm). For this method sow two seeds per 12 in (30 cm) of single row, spacing rows 2 ft 6 in (75–80 cm) apart. Although quite convenient for the 10 ft × 12 ft (3 m × 4 m) vegetable plot, beans grown this way trail in the soil and are often curled and splashed with soil when gathered, so where possible it is better to grown them up some form of support (see figure 68). Give added

NB: Spacing for double rows: 9 in. (23 cm) between plants, 18 in. (45 cm) between lines, 42 in. (106 cm) between double rows.

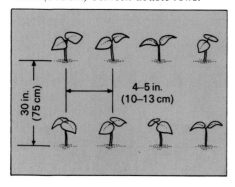

strengthening to cane and bean poles used to support a double row of runner beans by tying the tops of a few together, like wigwams (see figure 68). This will prevent the whole row blowing over on exposed sites should one support post break.

See that these plants never lack moisture. When the first flowers appear water regularly (every seven to ten days) with dilute liquid fertiliser and cover the surface of the soil with well-rotted compost or peat to retain moisture. This increases the yield. Syringing the leaves and flowers during hot weather helps the flowers to set and thus also increases cropping.

Harvesting

Pick regularly, at least twice a week when the beans are 10 in (25 cm) or more long. The more you pick the more beans the plants produce. You

will have greater chances of cropping well into the autumn by regular feeding and picking rather than making a second and later sowing. A double row along the 10 ft (3 m) length of the plot will provide at least two good pickings per week for a family of four from early August to early October.

Possible Problems

See under Dwarf French Beans.

Figure 69: Pinch out tips, and Runner Beans will grow without cane support.

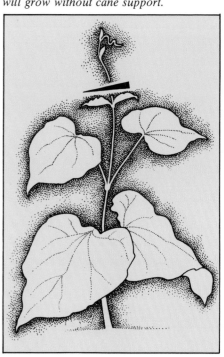

Beet

Whether boiled and preserved in vinegar to eat with salad, or eaten hot as an alternative to other root vegetables, the crimson globe beetroot (*Beta vulgaris*) is a most valuable vegetable which the home gardener can provide all the year round. Perhaps rather surprisingly it is the most popular of all seeds; there are more packets of red beet sold than any other single vegetable. Recent times have seen the introduction of golden beet, with such cultivars as 'Burpees Golden' which has orange skin and bright yellow flesh. These also have the added advantage of providing a dual purpose vegetable in that the leaves can be cooked and served like spinach.

Varieties

Take care when selecting varieties for early sowing (i.e. before April), because the ordinary globe kinds are likely to produce premature flower heads and run to seed (called bolting) rather than produce the globe shaped roots. Varieties like 'Avonearly' and 'Boltardy' have been bred to resist bolt-

Red Globe Beet.

Golden Beet.

ing and should always be used for early sowing.

Site and Soil

Any site, except those which are heavily shaded, and all well dug garden soils are suitable. Beet really thrives in hot, light – including sandy – soils.

Sowing Instructions

Each knobbly piece from the seed packet is in fact a cluster of seeds and not just one seed. Space these clusters 2–3 in (5 – 7 cm) apart down the row, 1 in (2·5 cm) deep with 9 – 15 in (23 – 38 cm) between the rows. If you intend to pull the roots as soon as they are golf ball size the closer row spacing is suitable. Sow at regular intervals to early July to provide a succession of tender young roots.

How to Grow

Single out the seedlings if more than one grow at each station. Apart from this just hoe occasionally to keep down weeds.

Harvesting

The tender young roots are the most delicious, so pull out every other plant as soon as the root is large enough. This spaces the remaining plants 6 in. (15 cm) apart and leaves ample room for full development of the later harvested roots.

Possible Problems

There are none.

USEFUL TIPS

1. A very light sprinkling of common salt, no more than ½ oz (14 gms) down 2 yds (1·8 m) of row, watered in, will improve growth and colour of the roots. You should be aiming to grow tender roots with no sign of woody white rings when the beet is cut in half. Plenty of moisture and the sprinkling of salt helps achieve this; shortage of moisture and slow growth makes the roots a bit on the woody and tough side and thus rather unpalatable.

2. When lifting beetroot always twist the leaves neatly from the root by hand rather than cutting with a knife. This leaves the roots ready for the pot once any soil has been washed off. Although cutting does no harm, twisting off is an easier way of removing the leaves, and avoids 'bleeding' – loss of sap.

3. Try growing such beetroot cultivars as 'Snow White', which has white roots. They actually taste very similar to the red types, but leave no red stains.

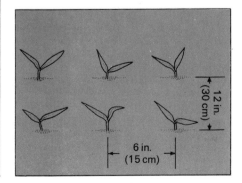

Long Beet.

Seakale Beet.

LONG BEET

Long beetroot is grown as a maincrop to lift and store for use throughout the winter. Both the very long-rooted kinds, like 'Cheltenham Green Top' which has green rather than the typical red leaves, and the cylindrical shaped kinds are convenient to the cook. They provide a good number of the same size rings from each root when sliced.

Site and Soil

Avoid heavy shade and freshly manured soils as the latter encourage plants to produce 'forked' roots, which are not ideal for culinary purposes.

Sowing Instructions

Sow the seed cluster 1 in (2·5 cm) deep and 3 in (7·5 cm) apart from late April to early June in rows 15–18 in (38–45 cm) apart. As the seedlings grow, thin them to 6 in (15 cm) apart.

How to Grow

Hoe occasionally to control weeds up to the stage where the leaves have grown sufficiently to cover the soil. No other treatment is necessary.

Harvesting

Lift maincrops in October to store in boxes of peat and sand (see figure 70) but be careful not to damage the succulent roots in any way. Roots lifted carefully and stored in a cool shed will provide you with beet right round to the earliest crops the following year.

SEAKALE BEET

There are white and red stemmed forms of seakale beet (*Beta vulgaris cicla*) commonly called 'Swiss Chard'. Both produce very attractive plants especially in late summer and early autumn when the bold leaves are very striking. The red leaved and stalked varieties, sometimes called 'Rhubarb Chard' are particularly beautiful.

Unlike other beet, seakale beet is grown, not for the root, but the leaves which are cooked like spinach, and the leaf stems which are cooked separately.

Sowing Instructions

Sow in the same way as long beet, in row 18 in (45 cm) apart. As the seedlings grow, thin them to stand finally at 8 in (20 cm) apart.

Figure 70: Store beet in peat or sand.

How to Grow

Hoe occasionally to control weeds.

Harvesting

Pull off the outer leaves as you require them. Inner younger leaves will develop to provide a succession.

Possible Problems

There are none.

USEFUL TIP

If you want to save space in the vegetable plot, you could grow a group of the red and white stemmed varieties in a circular patch in a herbaceous border, for example in front of phlox.

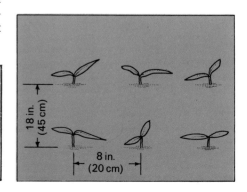

Broccoli and Cauliflower

In the past broccoli (*Brassica oleracea cymosa*) was the name used to describe the more hardy forms of white winter cauliflower as well as the 'Sprouting Broccoli' illustrated here. The current and perhaps less misleading practice is to restrict the name broccoli to the sprouting forms. Kales (*Brassica oleracea acephala*) have been linked with broccolis because the more recent types are similar in both their growing habit and culinary use. They also complete a year-round cycle of fresh green vegetable production from the garden.

Whilst green, purple and white sprouting broccolis and kale all require similar cultural treatment it is the green sprouting broccoli, (also called calabrese and the vegetable commercially sold in frozen form as broccoli spears), which starts off the cropping from midsummer to winter. The kales then take over and survive the toughest weather to provide fresh green vegetables through the winter and spring, to be followed by the white, the early purple and the late purple sprouting broccoli, which may be picked continually from early spring to early summer.

Those people who have found the kales rather strong flavoured should try recently introduced varieties such as 'Pentland Brig', a plant which produces many green shoots, and has a flavour that comes half way between kale and calabrese. When looking for kale in the seed catalogues, also look out for the synonyms – early kale and borecole.

Varieties

The purple sprouting broccoli, calabrese and kale like 'Pentland Brig' will give the maximum yield and therefore are particularly suitable for growing in the 10 ft × 12 ft (3 m × 4 m) vegetable plot. Choose early cropping F_1 hybrid calabrese which will be ready for cutting within six to seven weeks of planting out.

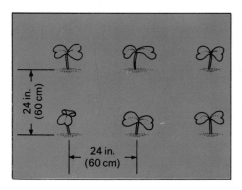

Site and Soil

The kales will stand very exposed conditions but choose a more sheltered site for the broccolis, and remember they form very large plants. Good, well cultivated soils are best and avoid freshly dug soil when planting out in early and midsummer. Plant out in well hoed soil between rows of early peas and broad beans for ideally suitable soil conditions.

Sowing Instructions

Sow seed in shallow drills ½–1 in (1–2·5 cm) deep, 6–9 ins (15–23 cm) apart in April and May. Plant out the resulting seedlings when they are big enough to handle (i.e. 4–6 in (10–15 cm) high) in the cropping site, 20–30 ins (50–75 cm) apart. Rows should also be spaced 20–30 in (50–75 cm) apart. You can plant out calabrese more closely (down to 12 × 9 ins (30 × 23 cm)) if you want to produce an abundance of small spears for deep freezing.

How to Grow

Water your plants in the seed row well and then pull them ready for dibbing out (see figure 71) into the cropping site. Stout growth is needed to withstand winter weather, so be sure the plants are well firmed to achieve this. You can check if they are firm enough after planting by holding a leaf between your finger and thumb and pul-

Purple Sprouting Broccoli.

White Sprouting Broccoli.

ling upwards. If a small piece of leaf tears away leaving the plant firmly in place, it is sufficiently firm. If the plant comes up from the soil with the leaf intact, you need to plant more firmly. When dibbing out, put the plant stems well down in the soil – this will improve the plant's anchorage and help it to withstand strong winds. The only other cultural treatment necessary is occasional hoeing to control weeds and watering in dry weather.

Harvesting

As the plants produce shoots and tips large enough to pick, start gathering and pick regularly, from then on. This

Calabrese.

grown repeatedly on the same soil without rotation, build up of the disease, club root, and the pest, cabbage root fly, is a possibility. You can achieve chemical control of these by dusting the *plant roots* with calomel for club root and by dusting the *soil* with either bromophos or a similar soil pesticide for root fly. Pick off by hand the green caterpillars of cabbage white butterfly should they occur, or spray the plants with derris. (For further information on these problems, see pages 112 and 115).

(For further information on these problems, see pages 112 and 115).

USEFUL TIPS

1. Water well with liquid fertiliser during hot, dry weather and then cover the surface soil with peat or well-rotted garden compost. This mulch retains moisture and also serves a useful purpose the following winter in keeping your shoes clean and reducing soil compaction as you pick the shoots in wet weather.
2. Plant the winter greens along the side of the plot next to the path, so that harvesting is an easier and cleaner job.
3. A dusting of garden lime hoed into the soil before sowing peas serves the peas well and also suits the succeeding winter greens crops.
4. Sprouting broccoli will live for several years but it is easier to start afresh each spring and better crops will be obtained by doing so.
5. Use chopped curly kale as an alternative to parsley for garnishing cooked dishes.

---

will be in April and May for sprouting broccoli, twelve months after sowing. The more you pick, the more new shoots will be produced. This is especially the case with sprouting broccoli, when, if you leave the first shoots to flower, the whole plant will turn woody and inedible. When gathering the sprouting broccoli, pick the larger centre spears first and don't discard the young leaves around the flower spears as these are quite as succulent as the flower buds. The purple flower buds of the purple sprouting varieties will turn rich green when cooked.

Possible Problems

All these plants are very easy to grow and generally trouble-free, but if they and other green crops (brassicas) are

Figure 71: Dib out young plants into the cropping site and test for firmness.

Kale.

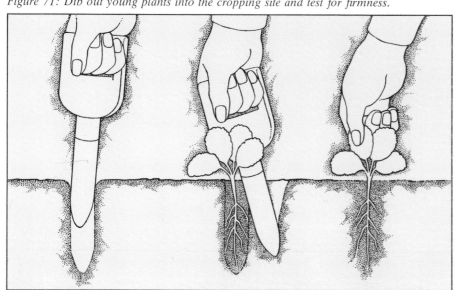

CAULIFLOWER

The name broccoli was traditionally given to white hearting cauliflower (*Brassica oleracea botrytis*) cultivars which were hardy enough to grow outside through the winter. Standardisation of names has now brought all types except Purple Sprouting Broccoli under the name cauliflower. Seed catalogues list a bewildering range of varieties of cauliflower, but success with this vegetable depends on working backwards from the date of maturity (for more details, see under CABBAGE, page 58). In all except the warmest, virtually frost-free areas, December- to March-maturing varieties are best avoided. In most cases, the varieties which mature from April to November will give satisfactory results, but remember that our cropping chart (see below) might vary a week or two either way according to the prevailing weather conditions. Summer-maturing cauliflower and hardy overwintered spring-maturing cauliflower (previously called winter broccoli) are the varieties most commonly grown in Great Britain.

Cauliflowers have the reputation of being difficult to grow, but in practice success depends on the quality of the soil. In good soils they are easy; in poor soils the gardener's skills are

Cauliflower.

fully tested and in this situation the spring-maturing varieties will often be the most successful.

Site and Soil

Select an open sunny site for all except the winter and early spring maturing kinds which will need some shelter from cold and cold winds. Cauliflowers grow best in well cultivated soils which you can further improve by adding plenty of very well rotted organic matter. This gives rapid growth and good sized 'curds', (the name given to the white cauliflower heads). If the soil is not chalky and alkaline, give it a dusting of lime. This is a help to all brassicas.

CAULIFLOWER CROPPING CHART					Harvesting			
Variety Examples	Sowing Date	Planting Out	Jan Feb	Mar Apr	May Jun	Jul Aug	Sept Oct	Nov Dec
Winter Hardy Varieties								
St George Summer Snow	May–June Outdoors	July–August		●	● ●			
Late Queen*					● ●			
Early Varieties Summer Maturing								
Dominant	Sow under cloches early October	March Sow direct				● ●		
Snowball*	Sow heated glass in Jan	April					● ●	
Le Cerf	March under glass	April/May				● ●		
Autumn Maturing (Australian Cauliflowers)								
Kangaroo*	Outdoors April/ May in succession for extended cropping	June/July					● ●	●
Snowcap							●	● ●
December–March Maturing for Coastal Areas and Sites with Mild Winters								
Roscoff Cauliflower								
Angers No. 2	Mid May	August	●	●				
St Hilary	Mid May	August	● ●	● ●				●
*Varieties to give cauliflowers from May to November.								

USEFUL TIP

Mini cauliflowers
Recent research work shows that very close planting of quick-maturing summer cauliflowers will yield mini cauliflowers. Spaced 6 in (15 cm) apart, the plants will yield small white hearts ideal for freezing, or delicious cooked straight after picking.

Figure 72: Fold outer leaves over to protect developing curds as cauliflower grows.

EARLY VARIETIES
Late Spring/Summer Maturing Cauliflowers

Sowing Instructions

Sow under cold glass in early October and in a heated atmosphere, even a warm window sill, in January. Transplant the small seedlings into pots as the third leaf (two round seed leaves will be followed by the third, which is rough-edged, and the first true leaf) appears. Handle seedlings carefully by the leaves when transplanting so as to avoid damaging the stem. Once established the potted seedlings need cold frame and cloche protection to produce sturdy plants. You can also sow seed outdoors in March/April to give successive summer crops.

How to Grow

Plant out in the cropping site 18 ins (45 cm) apart from March onwards. Hoe occasionally to control weeds. If cold, uncomfortable conditions cause a check to growth, turning the plants bluish-green, apply liquid fertiliser or hoe a nitrogen-giving fertiliser such as nitrate of soda or sulphate of ammonia into the soil around plants at the rate of 1 oz per 8 sq yd (30 gms per sq m).

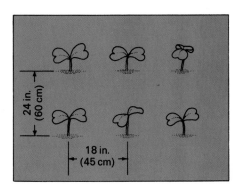

AUTUMN – Early Winter and Spring Maturing Cauliflowers (including the Australian cultivars)

Sowing Instructions

Sow outdoors in plant-raising rows in late April/May, the seed just covered, in rows 9 ins (23 cm) apart.

How to Grow

Water the plants well before lifting and transplanting in the cropping site in June/July. Leave 20–24 ins (50–60 cm) between plants and between rows. As the curds develop break the mid rib of a few large leaves and folding these outer leaves over the cauliflower head. This protects the head from soil splashes and keeps it beautifully white.

Harvesting

Rows of cauliflower have the habit of all maturing ready for harvest at the same time. When you have a surplus

you can store some temporarily by lifting mature plants and hanging them by the stalk in a cool shed. Syringe these lifted plants with water occasionally to keep them fresh for the longest possible period.

Possible Problems

The problems are generally the same as those under CABBAGE, but in addition a shortage of boron occasionally occurs in soils causing the leaves to grow narrow and turn brown. The cauliflowers will be bitter. Correct this by hoeing a dusting of borax into the soil. The correct proportions are 1 oz to 60 sq yd (30 gms to 50 sq m).

Spring Maturing Cauliflower, previously called Broccoli.

Brussels Sprouts

The key to producing quality crops of this popular winter vegetable (*Brassica oleracea gemmifera*) is to select hybrid varieties, from which you pick sprouts while they are small and firm.

Site and Soil
Sprouts are quite hardy and will grow in most sites, including partially shaded ones, and they require well cultivated soils which are firm at planting time.

Sowing Instructions
Sow under cover very early in spring for the earliest crops which will be ready from September onwards. Follow this with the main sowing outdoors in shallow drills 1 in (2·5 cm) deep and 6 in (15 cm) apart in March/April.

USEFUL TIP
Don't be in a hurry to pull up the stalks in spring. Instead pinch out the tops and pick any young shoots that develop during April and May. These cook as well as spring greens and sprouting broccoli.

How to Grow
Water the seedlings well before lifting and transplanting into the cropping site in May to early July. Use a trowel or dibber as described for broccoli. The earlier the plants are established, the bigger they will grow and the heavier the crop of sprouts they will yield. Hoe occasionally to destroy weeds until the leaves cover the soil and naturally smother weed growth. During very dry weather help growth by watering well and giving liquid fertiliser. This treatment is actually essential for some of the high yielding new F_1 hybrids.

Harvesting
Start snapping off the largest and lower sprouts as soon as they are big enough, (about 1 in (3 cm) in diame-

Brussels Sprouts.

ter). The flavour is best after a touch of frost. Remove yellowing leaves to make subsequent gathering easier.

The varieties that are especially bred to provide sprouts for freezing tend to crop all at once, and you can virtually pull up the plant to pick off all the sprouts. For general garden purposes the late varieties are preferable because they can be cropped over a much longer period, certainly from November to March.

Possible Problems
Plants subjected to dry conditions from late summer onwards are liable to be attacked by white fly. These are very easily controlled by spraying plants with the pesticides based on resmethrin, a chemical close to the natural pyrethrum. Sprouts from sprayed plants can be eaten within a day or so of spraying. Pick off the green caterpillars of cabbage white butterflies or spray with derris.

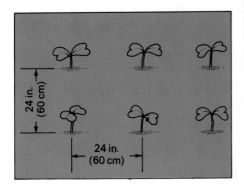

BRUSSELS SPROUTS CROPPING CHART										
						Harvesting				
Variety (Cultivar) Examples		Sowing Date	Aug	Sept	Oct	Nov	Dec	Jan	Feb	Mar
Early	Peer Gynt, F1	Sow under glass February Transplant April	●	●	●					
Mid to Late	Prince Askold, F1 Vremo Inter	Sow under glass early March and outside late March Transplant April/ May				●	●	●		
Late	Fasolt, F1	Sow early April outside Transplant May/June Also sow direct, no transplanting early May						●	●	● ● ●

(1) For the longest cropping period choose early, mid-season and late varieties (as per examples given above). Seasonal conditions will affect the cropping period and most varieties crop beyond the stated period.

(2) Where grown for freezing stop the plants by pinching out the growing tip when basal sprouts are ½ in (1 cm) diameter. This will help all sprouts to mature at once and allow ground to be cleared. Do not stop after September.

Cabbages and Savoys

Cabbages (*Brassica oleracea capitata*) and Savoys (*Brassica oleracea bullata*) cut fresh from the garden while still young and tender are quite unrecognisable in flavour from the tough old cabbages which have been cut and left on the greengrocer's shelf for several days before cooking. They are a very easy crop to grow, and whether you sow seeds to produce plants for transplanting or sow direct into the cropping position the attention they need is minimal.

It is very important to select varieties from the right group for any one time of year, much more so than to select an actual cultivar from the group. This is simple, as long as you make your selection by working back from the cabbages' maturity period. Thus in midsummer select and sow *spring cabbage*, in winter/early spring sow *summer cabbage* and in late spring/early summer sow *autumn* and *winter cabbage*.

Winter cabbages, especially the tight headed white cabbages and varieties like Celtic Cross F$_1$, are useful not only as a cooked vegetable but also chopped for use in salads.

Site and Soil
Most sites and just about all garden soils are suitable. In the very poorest soils and heavily overshadowed sites, cabbages may not produce very good hearts, but even under these conditions a summer sowing of spring maturing cabbage, given several good waterings with liquid fertiliser, will provide spring greens. Dusting the soil with lime for cabbage and other

Figure 73: Small cabbages will form on the stump of a cut cabbage.

Summer Maturing Cabbage.

brassica crops is advisable on all but chalky and limestone soils.

SUMMER MATURING CABBAGE
Sowing Instructions
Sow under glass (even indoors on the window sill) from mid-January to late February, and put the resulting plants outdoors from March onwards. Don't leave the early seedlings in too warm conditions for too long however, or they will become pale green, thin and sickly. Once they are up and well established with two or three leaves, it is best to put them under unheated glass or polythene. These sowings will provide the earliest cabbage in June.

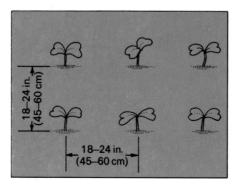

Sow outdoors in the open garden at regular intervals from April to May to provide a succession of cabbage through the summer.

How to Grow
The tender early plants raised under glass are soft and will need carefully planting with a trowel. Dib in the outdoor raised plants as for other brassicas (see Broccoli). Space plants 18–24 in (38–60 cm) apart with the same distance between rows. The larger you want the cabbage, the wider you should space the plants and rows apart.

Harvesting
Start to cut the cabbage as soon as the hearts begin to firm. If you wait until the hearts are fully developed the whole row will need cutting at once so it is better to start cutting early. In any event the young cabbage hearts are the most tasty.

SPRING CABBAGE
Sowing Instructions
Sow in shallow drills ½–1 in (1–2·5 cm) deep, the rows 6 in (15 cm)

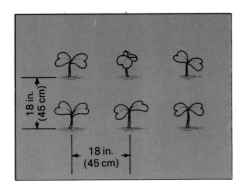

or so apart in late July. Water the resulting seedlings well before lifting and dibbing out in the cropping site in the autumn. If you miss the late July sowing, sow the seed direct in the cropping site in early August and then thin out when the seedlings are big enough to handle.

How to Grow
You should aim to get the young plants well established before the onset of winter. Spacing 6 in (15 cm) apart in the row allows you to cut every second and/or third plant while still immature as 'spring greens', sometimes called 'collards'. One row along the 10 ft (3 m) length of the vegetable plot will yield 3–4 lbs (1·35–1·8 kg) of spring greens by late April/early May,

Spring Maturing Cabbage.

with hearted cabbage ready by late May/early June. Space the rows 15–25 in (40–60 cm) apart. Once again the wider the spacing, the larger the cabbage will be, but the younger, smaller ones are still the best to eat.

WINTER CABBAGE AND SAVOYS
You can recognise the savoys easily by their large, thick, dark green leaves which have a bubbly-shaped surface. They are very easy to grow and a useful winter vegetable. Winter cabbage 'January King' has a reddish flush to the leaves covering the heart. If you want a bullet-hard cabbage heart which will stand in the garden fit to cut from January to April, try 'Celtic Cross' F_1.

Sowing Instructions
Sow in drills ½–1 in (1–2·5 cm) deep, 6–9 in (15–23 cm) apart in April/May. An earlier sowing gives a slightly earlier start to harvesting.

How to Grow
Water the seedlings well before pulling and dibbing out into soil which has been well cultivated for a previous crop, such as peas. Space the plants 15–24 in (40–60 cm) apart in the row, the rows 18–24 in (45–60 cm) apart.

Firm planting is advisable for these winter hearting cabbages.

RED CABBAGE
The very attractive deep reddish green cabbage is sown April/May and treated culturally like other summer cabbage. It is most often grown for pickling in vinegar, which turns the cabbage heart bright red, but it is also delicious if cooked fresh.

Possible Problems
The following problems are common to all cabbage types. Although they

Winter Maturing Cabbage.

occur quite often, they seldom prevent the harvesting of a crop, so they need not cause too much worry.

Caterpillars of cabbage white butterflies will eat holes into any cabbages from midsummer to late autumn and may be controlled either by crushing the eggs and picking off the caterpillars by hand or spraying with pesticides like derris and BHC.

Swollen knobbly roots are caused by the disease club root. Attack can be reduced or even prevented by dipping the plants in dust or paste of calomel. Don't grow brassica crops repeatedly on the same site or else diseases like club root will build up in the soil.

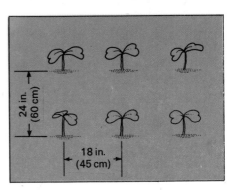

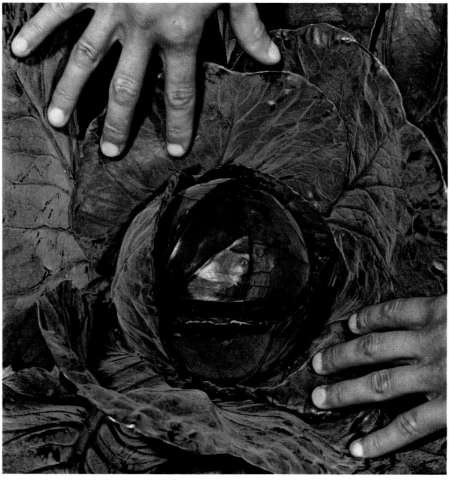

Red Cabbage.

Figure 75: Cabbage root fly.

watering well each evening or dusting the seedling with BHC. For maximum effect dust in early morning while the leaves still have the dew on them, so the BHC sticks to the dew and thus to the leaves.

Damage from pigeons, which eat the leaves in winter can only be controlled by erecting a temporary net. The other common problem is white aphid and white fly, which if allowed to, will work into the centres and hearts of your crop. Control as soon as you see them by spraying with

Small white maggots which are the offspring of cabbage root fly may eat the roots. Pull up plants that wilt in hot weather, and if you find these white maggots, destroy the plants, ideally by burning so as to eliminate this pest. If you know this pest occurs in your garden treat the roots with calomel dust or dip before planting them out into the cropping site you prepared.

You may notice neat round holes in the first two seedling leaves during periods of hot, dry weather; this may be particularly the case if you are growing the seedlings under cloches. The holes are eaten out by flea beetle which is easily controlled either by

Figure 74: Young cabbage seedlings and plants are particularly vulnerable to attack from pigeons, which, given the opportunity, will completely decimate a new crop. Protection can be given in various ways – (left) by enclosing seedlings with netting on all sides to form a pen. Pigeons will not fly down into this. Alternatively (right) they can be protected by erecting temporary netting to completely cover them.

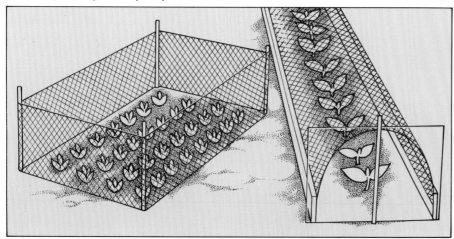

USEFUL TIPS

1. Growth can be speeded up by the application of nitrogen fertilisers. For example nitrate of soda or sulphate of ammonia, applied in early spring around spring maturing cabbage at up to 2 oz per square yard (75 gms per 1 sq m) will bring forward the harvesting period. Any of the common liquid fertilisers will also do this. For the fastest growth try watering or spraying with foliar fertiliser, (i.e. fertilisers which are absorbed through the leaves).

2. Foliar feed midsummer in dry weather helps winter maturing brassicas develop.

3. Leave the stumps after cutting spring maturing cabbage if green vegetables are in short supply because they will produce another crop of small cabbages.

4. To prevent cabbage root fly laying its eggs in the soil against the plant stem, make centre holes in discs of rubber carpet underlay 6–8 in (15–20 cm) across, slit radius and fit round plant stems.

Resmethrin, which is not harmful to humans and therefore harvesting need not be delayed for more than 24 hours after spraying.

CABBAGE – CHINESE

Chinese cabbage is a brassica but quite different in appearance to the other species. It is sometimes called by its common name 'Pe-Tsai', and looks more like a cos lettuce than cabbage. It has several culinary uses – it may be boiled in the same way as cabbage, but does not generate the typical cabbage smell when cooking and has a much milder flavour. Alternatively, the leaf ribs of outer leaves may be cooked like asparagus or seakale and the hearts may be shredded and used raw for salads.

Site and Soil

Chinese cabbage flourishes in similar sites to other cabbage crops. A soil improved by the addition of well rotted organic matter is essential to retain moisture.

Sowing Instructions

Sow direct in the cropping site in early July. It is better to sow and then thin out, as transplanting sometimes causes the plants to shoot up and form unwanted seed heads. Just cover the seed with soil and thin out the seedlings to stand 9–12 in (23–30 cm) apart, in rows spaced 12–15 in (30–38 cm) apart.

How to Grow

Make sure the plants do not lack moisture at the roots during hot weather. Otherwise just hoe occasionally to control weeds.

Possible Problems

There are none as long as you keep the plants growing strongly. F1 hybrid varieties will grow quite large for September harvesting.

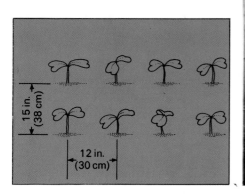

CABBAGES AND SAVOYS CROPPING CHART			Harvesting					
Variety Examples	Sowing Date	Planting Out	Jan Feb	Mar Apr	May Jun	Jul Aug	Sept Oct	Nov Dec
*Celtic Cross F1,	May	June–July	● ●	●				
Savoy Ormskirk	April/May	June–July	● ●	●				
*Wheelers Imperial (Spring maturing cabbage can also be cut as greens during this period.)	Late July	September			●	●		
Golden Acre (round) Greyhound (pointed)	Jan/Feb under glass	March–April				●		
*Gold Acre (round) Greyhound (pointed)	Early April	Thin out when ready					●	
Golden Acre (round) Greyhound (pointed)	Late April	Thin out when ready					●	
Golden Acre (round) Greyhound (pointed)	Mid May	Thin out when ready					●	
Winnigstadt	Late May	Thin out when ready					●	
*Christmas Drum Head	April	June/July						● ●

Sow 10–14 days earlier if plants shown to be thinned out are transplanted.
*Cultivars equal to these 4 sown at these times will provide cabbage the year round.

Chinese Cabbage.

61

Carrots

Carrots (*Daucus carota*) may all be bright orangy-red in colour, but owing to the modern varieties, you can now grow any number of different shapes! In fact the purist vegetable grower dedicated to producing the super long exhibition specimens is being left behind as more tender roots in shapes more suited to chopping, shredding and serving whole appear in seed form each year.

Breeding new varieties over recent years has been directed towards removing the woody yellow cores from carrot roots and this explains the terms 'red cored' and 'red cored improved' attached to some varietal names.

Figure 76: Different types of Carrot: from l. to r. top row: Round, Slender Nantes, Amsterdam types, Autumn King, Intermediate, Long type. Bottom row: Larger Nantes, Early Nantes, Chantenay.

A variety of Nantes type.

Varieties

Be adventuresome in the selection of carrot varieties, for they are all equally easy to grow. The small round carrots (see figure 76) are lovely cooked whole as are the young slender finger-long Amsterdam and Nantes types. The various maincrop varieties will all produce larger roots which may be left to grow and then lifted in the autumn to store through the winter. All varieties can, however, be lifted young for the best and most tasty roots and all can be left to grow to full size, before lifting and storing. The best way to grow carrots therefore is to sow them sufficiently thickly to allow you to pull some young whilst leaving others to get larger to provide the maincrop for storing.

Site and Soil

Only very heavily shaded sites cause difficulties in growing carrots and all garden soils will yield reasonable crops although ideally the soil should be of a lighter, sandy nature for the straightest, well shaped roots.

Sowing Instructions

Sow the earliest crops under glass and polythene in February, and follow with outdoor sowings as soon as soil conditions are suitable (i.e. not too wet or hard). It is better to delay sowing than to sow when the soil is cold, wet and too sticky under foot. Sow the seed in shallow drills ½–1 in (1–2·5 cm) deep and just cover it with soil. Space the rows 9–12 in (23–23 cm) apart: the wider spacing if you have plenty of room and want really big carrots. Make several regular sowings from March to July, (perhaps one a month), to give a succession of tender young carrots to pull throughout the season while still leaving sufficient to store for use in the winter.

A variety of Chantenay Carrot.

How to Grow

Thin the seedlings to stand 1 in (2·5 cm) or so apart. When they are large enough to handle, this will allow you to pull either every other, or every two in three, carrots from the stage when they reach finger thickness. Leave the remaining carrots to reach maincrop size. Hoe regularly between plants and rows to remove weeds, but be careful to keep the hoe blade away from the roots and so avoid cutting into the carrot. If your carrots do not grow as quickly as you would like, water the foliage with a foliar feed from time to time.

If you are growing carrots as a maincrop, with the intention of lifting the roots for use through the winter, make sure the 'shoulder' – that is the top of the root – does not grow out of the soil. This turns it green and inedible, but can be prevented by pulling a little soil up around the base of the leaf stalks.

Harvesting

Once again, I can't stress enough the

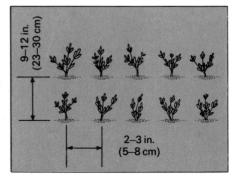

An early forcing type.

merit of pulling your carrots young for the best flavour. The earliest crops, pulled and shredded, are delicious raw in salads or boiled and served with butter. Lift maincrops carefully, easing them out of the soil with a fork or spade. Trim off the tops with a knife, then cover with sand, peat or loose soil and store in a shed or similar cool, dry storage place. Alternatively, leave them in the soil and lift as you require them.

Possible Problems

Carrot fly is the only problem you are likely to experience. The adult flies lay eggs in May/June and the second brood in July/August. The eggs hatch to produce small maggots which tunnel into the roots. The adult fly is attracted to the carrots by the smell released from fresh leaves and for this reason the seedling carrots should be handled as little as possible. It will help if you don't sow the seed too

A round rooted variety.

thickly, so you have fewer seedlings to thin out. Wilting leaves and the change of leaf colour from green to reddish shades are signs of attack. You can guard against carrot fly by working bromophos or diazinon granules into the soil at sowing time.

Roots will split when very dry weather is followed by heavy rain, so water the soil in dry periods to reduce the chance of this happening.

USEFUL TIPS

1. If you have had problems with carrot fly and don't like using chemicals, try 'Autumn King', which is more resistant to attack than other varieties.
2. Remember, very early crops can be lifted before the carrot fly maggots become active.

Figure 77: Thin seedlings when they are large enough to handle. Be careful not to spike the carrots when lifting.

Celery and Celeriac

There are four main groups of varieties under this heading, (*Apium graveolens*) all of which provide the subtle celery flavour and each serving a purpose in the supply of vegetables and salad. Most popular in Great Britain and certainly the best to eat for salads are the varieties which need blanching by drawing soil up round the leaf stems. There are white, pink and red stemmed varieties in this group.

Much less work to grow and with recently introduced varieties of improved quality, are the self-blanched kinds which have white stems and yellowish-green leaves. There is also the green, sometimes called American green, self-blanching celery which has green stems, rich green leaves and is very crisp and easy to grow. Both the self-blanching kinds are less hardy than the blanched types and need to be harvested before severe frost occurs and ruins the crops.

Finally there is celeriac, commonly and very descriptively called 'Turnip-rooted celery'. This plant produces a swollen root which may be cooked as a flavouring for soups and stews or shredded raw and eaten in salads. Celeriac considerably extends the fresh celery season as it may be lifted and stored well into the winter.

Site and Soil

Most garden sites are suitable, and a deeply dug, good soil is needed for the best results. Cultivate plenty of well-rotted organic matter into the soil ahead of sowing celery. This is especially necessary for blanched types; the self-blanching types are not quite so demanding and celeriac will crop well on poorer soils.

Sowing Instructions

Ideally sow all types under glass in spring, preferably mid-March/April, and make two sowings, one early and one late, to extend the cropping period. Earlier sowings of self-blanching celery will provide early crops.

Sow the seed in any seed compost, just covered, in a temperature of at least 50°F (10°C). When seedlings are just large enough to handle transplant them into boxes filled with potting compost or singly into 3½ in (9 cm) pots. Once established you can grow them under cloches, for transplanting into the cropping site in May/June.

How to Grow

Celeriac: draw out a deep drill and plant out in the base 9–12 in

Celeriac.

(23–30 cm) apart. The drill makes subsequent watering easier as growth and succulence is dependent on ample moisture. Space the rows 15–18 in (40–45 cm) apart. Hoe to control weeds, and remove side shoots which may develop to distort root shape. Also remove old yellow leaves as the plants develop.

Figure 78: Surround plants with cardboard before earthing up.

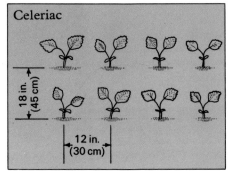

Celeriac

18 in. (45 cm)

12 in. (30 cm)

Self-blanching Celery.

Figure 79: Young plants established in the trench, ready for earthing up.

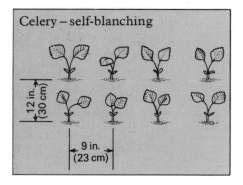

Celery – self-blanching

12 in. (30 cm)

9 in. (23 cm)

Celery – all self-blanching kinds: plant in a square block of several rows. The inner plants will become more blanched and better to eat than those growing in the outside and in single rows. Set out plants 9–12 in (23–30 cm) apart in both directions, using the wider spacing on the best soils where you can expect to grow very large plants. Once established, hoe in a general fertiliser at 1 oz per sq yd (33 gms per sq m) and water well in dry weather.

Tuck in some protective material such as wood wool, straw or old pea stems around the outside rows to help blanch the outer stems and bring them up to the quality of plants in the centre of the block. Such material will also give a little protection against frost if you wish to extend the harvest period.

Self-blanching celery is a very good summer crop for cold frames. Remove glass lights when the plants are well established in the base soil. The side walls will help blanch the plants in the outer rows.

Celery – which needs blanching; the traditional way to grow these cultivars is to dig trenches in spring which are one spade deep, 12–15 in (30–38 cm) wide and 3 ft (90 cm) apart. Dig well-rotted manure and/or compost into the base of the trench and leave it to settle before setting out the plants 6 in (15 cm) apart in the base of the trench in May/June.

Celery varieties which need blanching can be grown on the surface of the soil without trenching either by earthing-up like potatoes or by placing a wooden board on each side of the row and filling with peat. It is also a good idea to surround the plants with a collar of corrugated cardboard before you do any form of earthing (see figure 78). This holds the leaves together, preventing soil getting into the celery hearts.

You can begin the earthing up and blanching procedures when the leaves are 12–15 in (30–38 cm) high. Always leave the green leaves exposed and increase the height of blanching up the stem in stages over several weeks. Six to eight weeks at least will be needed to blanch stems and heart.

Once fully earthed up, the soil gives considerable frost protection to the plants and if you cover the leaves with straw and similar material as well, you can lift late maturing varieties from the soil into January and February.

USEFUL TIP

Celery tea is said to be a good medicinal aid to help rheumatism. Pour a pint (½ litre) of boiling water over 1 oz (25 gms) of seed to make the tea. *When using celery seed for medicinal and culinary purposes, be sure the seed has not been dressed with disease-preventing chemicals.*

Harvesting

Celeriac: plants can be pulled as soon as the roots are large enough. Generally they are lifted in October/November and stored in sand or peat for winter use.

Celery – self-blanching: lift as soon as the plants are large enough, usually from early September or earlier if grown under polythene.

Celery – blanched: many people claim the flavour is best after frost but you can begin to harvest this type of celery from September onwards – as soon as the inner heart is developed. When it is ready to lift remove the soil or

American Green Celery.

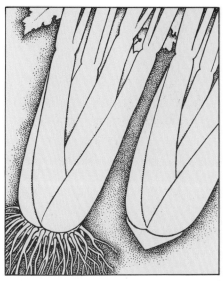

Figure 80: The white heart in the centre of the root is very succulent.

blanching material from around the stems as you want to lift the roots. Shake off the soil and cut off the loose fibrous roots with a sharp knife. Try to retain the white heart in the centre of the root however – it is one of the best pieces of blanched celery.

Possible Problems

Brown spots on the leaves, usually spreading in the autumn, are caused by celery leaf spot fungus. Protective seed dressing has considerably reduced the chance of infection (the better stocks of seed are already treated with Thiram when purchased) but you can control the disease, should it occur, with sprays of bordeaux mixture or maneb or zineb based materials.

Celery fly or leaf minor may cause trouble and you can identify by brown blisters which appear on the leaves from May. Pick off infected leaf parts and pinch to destroy the small larvae which tunnel between the two surfaces of the leaves. Where attacks persist treat with malathion spray.

Slugs can be a problem with earthed up celery. Try growing on flat ground and surrounding the stems with dryish peat to discourage these pests.

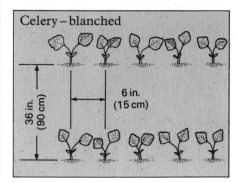

Celery – blanched

36 in. (90 cm)

6 in. (15 cm)

Chicory and Endives

Shredded chicons make good salad ingredients.

Forced roots at harvest time.

The plump, cream and white forced shoots of chicory (*Cichorium intybus*), called 'chicons', provide succulent, crisp salad in winter. The young blanched leaves are superb for mixed salads, to eat with cheese as a light snack, mixed with prawns and french dressing as an appetiser or as an additional sandwich filling. Chicons can also be wrapped in bacon and braised.

Chicory growing in mid-summer.

Left in the ground a second year, chicory produces sky blue flowers which are attractive in an herbaceous border.

Site and Soil
Pretty well all garden sites are suitable, but avoid those that are very heavily shaded. All well cultivated soils are suitable, but it is best to grow them in soils which have had manure and well-rotted compost added for previous crops. Raising chicory in freshly manured soils or soils which dry out considerably in summer encourages twisted forked shoots which are not easy to fit into containers.

Sowing Instructions
Sow the varieties 'Witloof' or 'Brussels' in rows in the garden in April/May, just covering the seed with soil. Single out the seedlings to the correct distance apart (i.e. 2–3 in (5–7·5 cm) for F_1 hybrid varieties, and 6 in (15 cm) for 'Witloof') as soon as they are large enough to separate easily with your fingers. Space the rows 15–18 in (40–45 cm) apart; (the wider spacing for 'Witloof').

How to Grow
Hoe occasionally to kill weeds and in very dry weather give a few heavy waterings to help to swell the roots.

Harvesting
When the leaves start to turn yellow in October/November and before there is a hard frost, lift the roots with a spade or fork. Holding the root in one hand twist off the leaves with the other and cut or snap off the thin root end to give plump roots 8 in (21 cm) long. Store these roots in a box of dry peat or sand in a cool, frost-free place.

From December to March put five or six roots upright in an 8 in (21 cm)

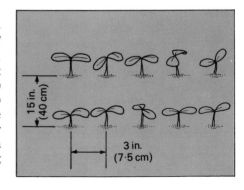

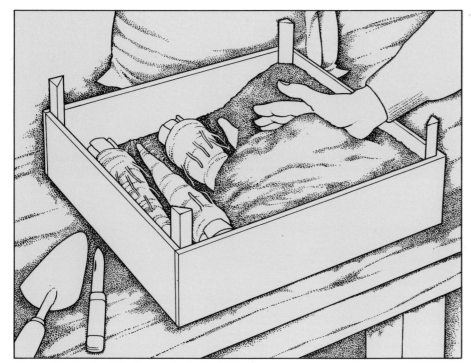

Figure 81: Storing lifted roots for later forcing.

usual practice to discard the roots, but if you re-cover them immediately, it is possible to harvest a second crop of thin leaves. Bring a few roots into the warm each week to provide a succession of chicons.

Possible Problems
There are none.

diameter flower pot (more roots can be placed in a larger container such as a wooden box), packing damp sand, light soil or peat around and over the roots to give them a fairly deep covering. Invert a size larger pot and cover the holes. Keep the soil moist and in a temperature of 50°F (10°C), and every root will form a chicon in approximately three to four weeks. Warmer temperatures will give faster growth but keep the soil damp and the shoots completely dark – light turns the leaves green and bitter tasting.

Pick the chicons by just snapping them from the root. After this it is

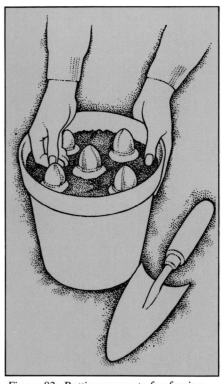

Figure 82: Potting up roots for forcing.

Roots in the foreground are forced, to produce the chicons seen on the left.

USEFUL TIPS

1. Watch out for F₁ hybrids like Normato (early), Mitado (Mid-season) and Tardivo (late). Normato can be forced in November/January, Mitado January/February and Tardivo in March/April to get a long cropping period. The F₁ hybrids do not need their roots covering with soil when forcing – instead put a one size larger flower pot upside down over the 8-in (21 cm) root filled pot. It is of course necessary to surround the roots in the pot with some peat, sand or damp soil, which must subsequently be kept moist. Smaller roots of the F₁ hybrids are fine and the closer spacing of 2–3 in. (5–7 cm) apart in the rows makes them ideal for the 10 ft (3 m) long rows of the vegetable plot.
2. Damp peat, ideally potting compost, used to pack round roots when forcing, can be used for several batches.

Endive.

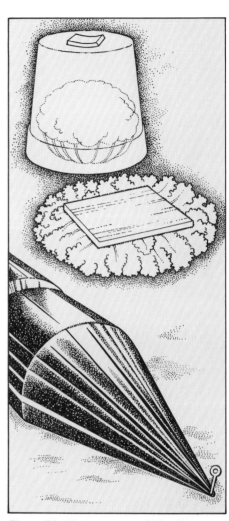

Figure 83: Various ways of blanching.

ENDIVE

Perhaps more popular in France than Britain, endive (*Chichorium endivia*) is a useful salad crop especially in early winter when lettuce crops have ended everywhere, except in heated greenhouses. It is often listed in seed catalogues with lettuce and chicory, but as the Latin name indicates it is really correct to place it with chicory as it is a member of the same family. There are two main types of endive – the Batavian type, which resembles a cos lettuce, and the curled type, which has divided and curled leaves.

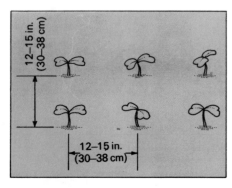

Site and Soil

All garden sites and any well-cultivated garden soil are suitable. Soils which have been improved over several years by adding well-rotted manure and compost will give the best results.

Sowing Instructions

Take a chance on sowing in April to provide a summer crop, but choose one of the curled leaf varieties for this. You will, however, obtain more successful crops from sowings of the hardy 'Winter Lettuce Leaved', (otherwise known as Batavian), type in late June to early August to mature in the winter. Sow in rows 12–15 in (30–38 cm) apart, where you want the crops to be, as both the check caused by actual transplanting of seedlings and dry weather affecting the early sown crop can cause the plants to form seed heads prematurely.

How to Grow

Thin the seedlings to stand 12–15 in (30–38 cm) apart (the wider spacing

for the main sowing). Hoe occasionally to control weeds and apply a top dressing of nitrogenous fertiliser or liquid feed to encourage the desired rapid growth.

Harvesting

When the plants are well developed either cover with an upturned flower pot or place a square of light board over the centre of the plant. This blanches the leaves over a period of three to six weeks according to speed of growth and makes them more succulent and less bitter to taste. If you cover winter crops with polythene tunnels, use black polythene as this will blanch the plants.

You can extend cropping by lifting the plants carefully, planting them in boxes of soil and storing them in a dark and frost-free shed. The frost protection extends the life of these plants and the darkness does the blanching.

Possible Problems

None so long as you encourage rapid growth in summer (see How to Grow).

Cucumbers

CUCUMBERS under cover

The long smooth skinned cucumbers (*Cucsumis sativus*) sold in the shops all the year round are varieties suited to growing in greenhouse, frame and, at a pinch, cloche conditions. They really demand a warm 65°F (18°C), moist atmosphere and, given this, they will grow very fast and crop heavily.

Site and Soil

It is necessary to have a greenhouse, lean-to sun lounge, cold frame or polythene tunnel house to grow these cucumbers. The growing medium needs to contain a considerable amount of organic material, and in fact fertilised peat-filled growing bags are one of the simplest ways to grow cucumbers in domestic situations, particularly if you want no more than two or three plants. One strong, well-grown plant will produce more than ten good cucumbers.

If you have access to strawy manure, build a bed of several 4–5 in (10–12·5 cm) layers of manure, and good garden soil or loam up to 2 ft (60 cm) capping finally with soil.

Sowing Instructions

Sow single seeds in 3½–4¼ in (9–11 cm) pots half filled with seed compost, any time from January to April. Remember 64°F (18°C) temperature is required for these plants. If sowing in unheated structures, delay sowing until April. The seed germinates very quickly, given sufficient warmth, and once the first two leaves open above the rim, fill up the pot with further compost. The cucumber is stem rooting and more roots will be made into the new compost.

How to Grow

When the stems are about 9–12 in (23–30 cm) long, the plants will be ready to plant out in the cropping site. Provide support for plants grown in greenhouses, either with canes or wires. As the main stem of the cucumber develops, tie it carefully to the cane or string. As it reaches the top of the cane, pinch out the growing tip. Side shoots (laterals) will then develop – pinch the growing tip out, either two leaves past the first fruit or certainly once the stem is 18–24 in (45–60 cm) long. Stop sub-laterals completely after one or two leaves have formed. Leave these side growths to hang or tie them to cross wires or a net-like backing support.

Watch for the two kinds of flower to

Outdoor Ridge Cucumbers.

form – the male flowers have just a simple stem and should be removed; and the female flowers which have an immature cucumber behind the flower. If you leave the male flowers on the plant and bees cross-pollinate, you will get misshapen bitter cucumbers as a result.

If you are growing the cucumbers in frames, you don't need to provide support but you should pinch them out in a similar way. Stop the first main stem at six to eight leaves or when the plant reaches across the frame. Stop side shoots at two leaves past the first fruit,

Frame Cucumbers.

or when they are 18–24 in (45–60 cm) long. Keep the sub-laterals which develop very short and remove them altogether when the frame becomes too densely filled with foliage. Lift fruits on frame-grown plants and place them on a piece of wood or tile to keep them clean. Give the plants liquid feed every ten to fourteen days when the first fruits have started to swell.

USEFUL TIPS

1. Select F₁ hybrid 'all female' flowering varieties to avoid the problems of cross pollination. These varieties need temperatures of 65–70°F (18–21°C).
2. Mulch mid summer with potting compost 3–4 in (7·5–10 cm) deep around the stem to encourage new root growth and more cucumbers.
3. Avoid growing cucumbers in the same greenhouse soil one year after another.

Harvesting

Cut as soon as the cucumbers have reached full length and have swollen nicely. Don't leave them until they start to turn yellowish-green.

Possible Problems

Keep the greenhouse regularly sprayed with water to encourage plant

Figure 84: Diagrammatic explanation of cucumber training under glass. Laterals and sub-laterals are tied to cross wires.

Cordon-trained cucumbers in a greenhouse – note how sub-laterals are left to hang.

growth. It will also help to reduce the likelihood of attack by Red Spider Mite as this pest likes a hot, dry atmosphere. Red Spider Mites turn cucumber leaves yellowish-bronze rather than rich green.

When the temperature is warm enough and growth rapid, problems are few.

OUTDOOR CUCUMBERS AND GHERKINS

Look for seed marked 'Ridge Cucumber' and 'Outdoor Cucumber' for the easiest cucumbers to grow, either unprotected outdoors or under cloches. *Gherkins*, are grown in just the same way as ridge cucumbers.

Site and Soil

A well rotted compost heap in a sheltered, sunny position is ideal for ridge

Figure 85. Male and female flowers.

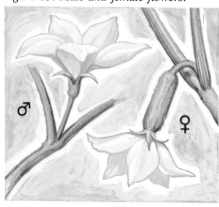

cucumbers. Alternatively plant in a sunny sheltered site and in soil which you have improved by adding plenty of very well rotted organic matter.

Sowing Instructions

Either sow indoors in pots in April/early May or outside under cloches in the cropping site in mid-May/early June. If raising indoors sow two seeds per pot and thin to one as soon as the seedlings are large enough to handle. Plant out 3–4 ft (90–120 cm) apart in late May/early June and *after* the chance of frost if cloche protection is not available. You can also sow two or three seeds at each station outdoors and thin down to the strongest plant once established.

USEFUL TIP

It is advisable to plant all cucumbers on a small hill of compost or soil to prevent water resting around the stem. While they like plenty of moisture in the atmosphere and in the rooting area, they will not stand waterlogged conditions.

How to Grow

Let the plants run and give occasional liquid feeds and plenty of water in dry weather. Although it is not essential, it is best to stop the main stem at six to eight leaves, thus encouraging the side shoots to develop.

Be sure to *retain* the male flowers on

ridge cucumbers. Cross pollination is essential in these plants and some hand fertilisation, (i.e. taking the male flower, removing the petals and placing the pollen-bearing parts in the mouth of the female flower) will help to set fruit.

Put a piece of glass or wood under developing cucumbers to keep them clean.

Harvesting

Cut the fruits as soon as they are large enough – the more you cut the more the plant will produce. One well grown plant will yield sufficient cucumbers for one or two people from late July up until frost occurs.

Possible Problems

Watch for slugs at the early stages. If plants are allowed to get dry, mildew (a greyish growth on the leaves) is likely to occur. Use a systemic fungicide to control this.

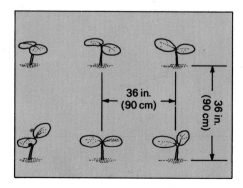

Herbs

A number of herbs make very attractive plants in their own right. The stately evergreen bay, the powder blue flowers of rosemary and the ground-covering purple and cream variegated sage provide excellent examples. It is their attractive and appealing aromatic flavours which bring them into happy partnership with vegetables however, and all vegetable gardeners should find some space to grow herbs. They can be grown in between vegetables in the plot or away from it altogether as a small herb border.

The strongest flavours will be produced by plants that are grown in full sunlight and well-drained soils. Don't worry too much if you are unable to provide the ideal conditions, however, because in practice the common herbs will grow easily in all soils although heavy wet soils make for a short life in some herbs (two to three years).

Most people require small quantities of herbs for flavouring – a sprig of mint for new potatoes and a sprinkling of chives for cream cheese for example. For this reason it is convenient if plants are situated close to the kitchen door. A few plants grown in pots, window boxes or tubs placed near the back door will prove very handy and herbs used fresh will yield up maximum flavour.

Taking the convenience aspect even further, a few selected plants can be grown indoors on the window sill,

Figure 87: Formal trained Bay Trees. (Above) Bay tree growing without root restriction.

Figure 86: Herbs grown in strawberry pots.

either in small troughs or in hanging plant containers. The perennial kinds like mint, sage and thyme are good for this, and so is parsley, although if it is close to hand you will find yourself using it so often you will soon need to replace it!

Don't be afraid to pinch the shoots of most herbs regularly. Plants such as sage and thyme will grow away again strongly after each pinching and produce more compact and bushy plants as a result.

BAY

Fresh and dried leaves of this evergreen (*Laurus nobilis*) are used combined with other herbs in a bouquet garni and on their own to flavour many dishes. Although it is a hardy evergreen, try to avoid exposure to cold easterly winds which burn back the leaves.

Over the years bay will grow into a small tree, but it also responds to pot culture, either as a low bushy plant, possibly trimmed to a pyramid, or grown on a stem to form the typical standard 'round-headed' plant seen in tubs outside restaurants. Shaped plants will need trimming with secateurs two or three times a year to retain their shape, but don't use shears as these cut the leaves in half.

Plants grown in pots are best taken into a light garage or an outbuilding for protection in the depths of winter.

You can obtain new plants by rooting young tips when stems start to harden in July/August. Once well rooted, grow on in potting compost and then plant in the garden when they are well established (September and March/April are good times to plant in the open garden).

Leaves can be dried for future use in several ways, the easiest being to place several in a shallow tray in a very cool oven. Dried leaves are likely to have a stronger flavour than leaves which are gathered for use fresh.

CHIVES

Grassy chive (*Allium schoenoprasum*) foliage is easy to grow from seed, and chopped into small pieces it gives a delicate onion flavour to salads, egg dishes, cream cheese, soups and sauces. Sow at any time of the year, but to get the strongest growing plants, sow early in the year so the plants develop slender bulbs.

Clusters of bulbs along the edge of a path will produce all the foliage you will need during spring and summer but if you want fresh supplies all the year, grow a few seed-raised crops indoors.

Chives flourish in a shaded border, and once plants are established cut them back to the soil regularly to encourage new growth. Lift and divide established clumps every few years in April or September. Cut off flower heads as they appear.

The bright green colour is lost if the leaves are dried and it is much better to either keep supplies of fresh leaves coming along or deep freeze some.

Chives.

DANDELION

Dandelion (*Taraxacum officinale*) can be classed as a herb as its roots may be roasted and ground to make either a coffee substitute or additive. Alternatively it may be grown as a vegetable – to use the leaves raw in salads (the large-leaved varieties available from specialist seedsmen are particularly suitable), cooked like spinach or used as a flavouring for soups, for example, like sorrel. Unlike most other herbs, however, it likes a shady spot and a moist fertile soil if it is to produce large leaves.

Sow it in spring (April is a good month) in small groups and thin the plants as they grow to stand 6 in (15 cm) apart. Blanch them the following spring with an upturned pot or box. This will give you a succession of blanched leaves for salads. After blanching and picking the leaves, give the plants a rest to rebuild their vigour before blanching a few more leaves.

If you wish to use the roots of dandelion, you can harvest them at any time after the growth has begun to slow down in the autumn. For the biggest, most succulent roots, however, leave the plants until the foliage has really stopped growing in the late autumn, early winter (October/November).

Dandelion.

Dill.

DILL

This plant (*Anethum graveolens*) is grown for its thin feathery foliage. It is an annual, so must be raised each year from a spring sowing. Give it a fair amount of room, because plants will grow to 3 ft (90 cm) in height. If you are growing several plants space them 9–12 in (23–30 cm) apart.

Both leaves and seeds give a flavour akin to caraway and aniseed, but use them sparingly because the flavour is quite strong. Use chopped leaves to flavour soups, sauces and savoury stews and add seeds to vinegar to produce dill vinegar for pickled gherkins. Try sprinkling a little seed over sliced cucumber in sandwiches.

Florence Fennel.

FENNEL

There are two plants with the common name 'fennel' – the perennial *Foeniculum vulgare*, common fennel, grown only for the foliage to use as a herb and *Foeniculum vulgare dulce*, the Florence fennel or finocchio which has similar feather foliage but is also grown for the swollen leaf bases, which may be eaten raw in salads or cooked to flavour stews.

Sow common fennel in March/May in rows 15 in (38 cm) apart. If you want seed heads to develop so as to use the seed for herbal purposes, go for the early sowing. Thin the seedlings to stand 12 in (30 cm) apart. Established plants can be divided in spring – as with chives. Leaves cannot easily be stored so either deep freeze some or pot up some plants to grow indoors to provide winter flavouring. Cut seed heads in September and October and hang them upside down in paper bags to dry. Seeds soaked in water are said to make a good soothing liquid for stomach ache.

Sow Florence fennel in April in rows 20 in (50 cm) apart and thin the seedlings to 9–12 in (23–30 cm) apart. Put them in warm, well-drained soil in a sunny position. As the leaf bases start to swell, hoe soil up around them to give the blanched white colour.

GARLIC

Although garlic (*Allium sativum*) is used as a flavouring it is in fact a form of onion and can be grown in just the same way as shallots and onion sets. Divide a bought bulb into cloves and plant these 6 in (15 cm) apart in rows 12 in (30 cm) apart. Plant in October

Garlic.

for harvestable bulbs in July/August, and in March for bulbs in October. Lift the bulbs when the leaves start to yellow and put them in trays to dry.

If you protect the growing bulbs with polythene tunnel cloches you will get a much better finished bulb. Garlic cloves should be crushed, not chopped, for use in cooking. Rub round a salad bowl with a crushed clove to give a subtle garlic flavour.

HORSERADISH

Shredded slivers from the white cylindrical roots of horseradish (*Armoracia rusticana*), used fresh in cream sauces provide the traditional, hot mustardy flavoured relish to go with roast beef. The fresh root scrapings can also be used to flavour fish and other dishes to give a pungent flavour.

Any small piece of root will grow, but the top crown-shooting part (which is unusable for culinary purposes) is best. Plant in spring, 18 in (45 cm) apart, but plant sparingly because once established the deep

searching thongy roots soon become very invasive and take some digging out. Leaves will grow 2 ft (60 cm) or so high. Lift the roots from November and store in sand and peat for use when the soil is frozen.

Horseradish roots cut to make planting thongs.

MARJORAM – sweet

Used in mixed herbs with thyme or as an alternative flavouring to thyme, 'Sweet Marjoram' (*Origanum marjorana*) is actually a perennial. However it is best treated as an annual in Britain as it will die outdoors in winter in all but the most sheltered spots.

Sow the seed under glass in March and plant out the seedlings in late May/early June 9–12 in. (23–30 cm) apart in a warm sunny position. Alternatively, sow direct into the cropping position in mid-April. Gather the leaves as they get large enough and before the plant develops flower heads. Chop them for use fresh and dry some for winter supplies.

Mint. Figure 88: (right) To get early mint, grow indoors in a pot.

Marjoram.

For a stronger flavour and to provide fresh leaves in winter grow 'Pot Marjoram', *Origanum onites*, of which there are two types, a green-stemmed, white-flowered form and purple-stemmed and flowered form. More attractive but used in a similar way is the golden-leaved *Origanum aureum*. Pot marjoram is a hardy perennial but needs a warm position if grown in the garden. Sow seeds in April or September in drills 12 in (30 cm) apart. Thin the seedlings or transplant them 12 in (30 cm) apart.

MINT

The 'Common Mint' (*Mentha spicata*) or 'Spearmint' (as shown in the photograph) is the species most frequently found in gardens and is most recommended for mint sauce, although there are more than six kinds frequently listed in catalogues. Another type worthy of note is *Mentha rotundi-folia*, the round-leaved or 'Apple Mint', a type not affected by the disease rust and claimed by many as the best to use with new potatoes. There is a very attractive white variegated form of apple mint.

The growth of mint usually needs restraining rather than encouraging, and a good tip is to plant the pieces of root, from which new plants are grown, in an old plastic bucket, or similar container with a hole in the base. Bury this in the garden to within 2 in (5 cm) of the rim and fill it with soil. Mint roots are then contained and do not spread all over the garden.

Parsley.

Lift some roots in the autumn and grow them in pots indoors to supply young sprigs in winter and early spring.

PARSLEY

Parsley (*Petroselinum crispum*) is one of the most useful of all our herbs – ideal for garnishing, in sauces and stuffings and as a constituent of bouquet garni. It is a biennial plant which will produce leaves for several seasons if the flowering stems are cut out before they fully develop. It is available in several varieties which vary in the degree of curling and cut edges to the leaves.

Sow the seed in rows 9–12 in (23–30 cm) apart in spring for summer and autumn use and late July/early August for winter use. Thin the seedlings to stand 6–12 in apart (15–30 cm). Protect the winter crop with cloches.

Parsley seed is slow to germinate and the old cottage gardener's tip of pouring boiling water along the drill sometimes speeds germination. Avoid germination failure by not using old seed. Parsley will stand some shade and produces a lot more leaf if it is given the occasional liquid feed. Fresh leaves are by far the best, but you can ensure additional winter supplies by air-drying bunches of foliage in summer and rubbing it down before storing in sealed jars. To retain the colour

Rosemary. Figure 89: (below) Plant cuttings of rosemary or thyme in sandy soil.

dip fresh leaves in boiling water for a minute or so, shake dry and then dry quickly in a cooling oven.

ROSEMARY

You can raise the shrubby evergreen Rosemary (*Rosmarinus officinalis*) from seed sown in spring and summer or by propagating from cuttings in August, September and October. Lighter soils give best results and although it is a virtually hardy plant, very severe frost and cold, or easterly winds will destroy the branches. New growth will often come through again from the base where the plants have been damaged by frost. Rosemary responds well to pot growing.

Try to find a space towards the front of a small shrub border. Plants will grow quite large and will spread, but to no more than 2–3 ft (60–90 cm) high if trimmed back in spring to keep tidy. There are some very attractive gold and silver variegated forms, but these are not as strong growing as the green types.

SAGE

Sage (*Salvia officinalis*) is another shrubby herb and as well as the true species with its attractive greyish-green leaves, there are purple-green and cream, and pink and green variegated forms. All make attractive low shrubs and can be used as ground cover in a purely decorative role.

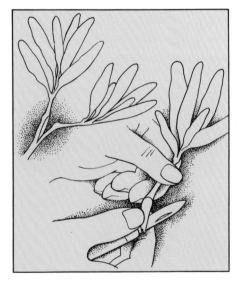

Sage.

Young plants will yield the most useful flavoured foliage in well-drained soil and a warm sunny site.

Plants from all species can be raised easily from seed sown from March to June. Propagate from cuttings rooted in sandy compost in September.

Trim off the purple flowers before they open. Cut plants back to get a harvest of shoots and also to encourage more basal growth and foliage. Plants also become rough and untidy looking if not regularly trimmed back. The rather woody stems and thick leaves gathered for storing take quite a long time to dry. Keep them in a warm, airy place and once dry just rub the leaves in your hands to break them up. Store in an airtight jar. One good bush cut over twice in a season will provide quite enough sage for a year's use.

THYME

Common garden thyme (*Thymus vulgaris*) is a really attractive plant. Used as a low decorative shrub and planted close to the path or near the back door, you will be aware of the delicious thyme fragrance every time you brush by. Young shoots need cutting to dry for herb use, but if left, the 8–12 in (20–23 cm) plants are covered with pretty purple flowers in June. There are very many thyme species, among them a golden-leaved form, *Thymus vulgaris* 'Aureus'. Another particularly attractive type is the lemon thyme, *Thymus x citriodorus* which has silver and golden-leaved forms.

Choose a sunny site and light, sandy soil for these plants. Propagate by cuttings taken with a heel in May/June or raise common thyme by sowing seed any time from March to July. Once established, put out young plants in the garden 9–12 in (23–30 cm) apart or grow in pots and window boxes.

Thyme.

Kohl Rabi and Swedes

The kohl rabi (*Brassica caulorapa*) is an interesting and attractive plant to grow. Its swollen stem, which looks like a 'root', can either be cooked or sliced raw to eat in salads, and it tastes like a mixture of turnip and cabbage. Red or green coloured varieties are available.

Swedes (*Brassica napobrassica*) are sometimes confused with turnips but they are in fact larger and sweeter. The one-time practice of field-growing great big swede roots and selling them as vegetables when they were actually more suited to cattle food, has happily largely been replaced by the more enlightened approach of growing smaller roots for home use. Both swedes and kohl rabi are very useful root vegetables, and swedes can be stored like potatoes to use right through the winter.

Site and Soil

Pretty well any site, as long as it is not too overshadowed or dry, and any well-cultivated garden soil are suitable for both vegetables.

Sowing Instructions

Sow kohl rabi any time from March to early August, and for a succession of crops, sow two or three batches over this period. Sow swede in May or June. Space seed rows 15 in (38 cm) apart and thin seedlings to stand 6–9 in (15–23 cm) apart in a row. The smaller roots at the closer spacing, lifted while young, are the best to eat.

Swede.

How to Grow

Dust acid soils with lime before sowing. Other than this just hoe occasionally to destroy weeds and water well, ideally with some liquid fertiliser, in very dry weather. If plants experience a check in growth because of dry conditions, they will tend to be woody and less palatable.

Harvesting

Both crops can be pulled and used as soon as they are large enough, that is from about 2½–3 in (6–7.5 cm) in diameter. If the kohl rabi gets much more than 3½–4 in (9–10 cm) across it is likely to become woody in the centre. Later sowings of kohl rabi can be pul-

led and stored in sand or peat to use into the winter. Where frost is not too severe the swede could be left in the ground and used as required.

Possible Problems

Pretty well trouble-free. Club root can attack these crops and control is the same as for cabbage. Sow swede in late May in the South of England to avoid getting mildew on the leaves in late summer.

USEFUL TIP

To time the kohl rabi sowing, remember it is ready to pull in twelve weeks, given reasonable seed germination conditions. Sown early and widely spaced, swedes will grow to a large size and are super for children to carve out into faces for Hallowe'en. The long columnar stump which carries the leaves forms the neck and the flesh glows pink if lit inside with a candle.

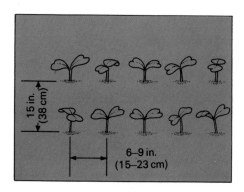

15 in. (38 cm)

6–9 in. (15–23 cm)

Green Kohl Rabi.

Red Kohl Rabi.

Leeks

Leeks (*Allium porrum*) are really tough, hardy plants which will survive hard frost and are thus a useful winter vegetable. They are members of the onion family and one of the easiest to grow. When plants grow strongly they produce masses of vigorous white root which breaks up heavy soil and, after lifting, leaves soil much more crumbly and friable. If your garden soil is heavy and tends to stay in great lumps, try growing a patch of leeks (as well as adding plenty of well-rotted organic matter) to improve the texture of the soil.

Site and Soil
Most sites, except those which are heavily shaded, and all well-cultivated soils are suitable.

Sowing Instructions
Sow early in the year, in February/March, under cover to get the earliest and largest blanched stems. An outdoor sowing in March/April will provide adequate crops, however. Transplant early seedlings into the cropping site in May, and the outdoor raised plants in June and even into July. Space plants 9 in (23 cm) apart in the row, the rows 12–15 in (30–38 cm) apart. Closer spacing produces smaller roots which are easier to handle in the kitchen.

How to Grow
Water the indoor seedlings and those in rows outdoors well before transplanting. Use a dibber to make a good hole 1 in (2.5 cm) or more in diameter, 6–8 in (15–20 cm) deep, drop the young plant into this and water it in. There is no need to fill back any soil, the effect of watering is sufficient to cover the roots with soil and the space allows some room for blanched stem development before hoeing and weathering fills in the hole. When lifting the seedlings from outdoor rows they are easier to handle if you shorten the leaves by a third, cutting them

Figure 90: Use a dibber to plant out. (Above) Leeks being harvested.

back level with a knife. Leave them long enough to just reach the top of the hole as you drop them in.

Control weeds by hoeing between the rows and apply a dilute liquid fertiliser in dry weather. When hoeing, draw soil up round the stem a little at a time to lengthen the blanched stem, but not so high that it goes over the point where the leaf joins the stem because if soil gets into the blanched stem the leeks are gritty.

USEFUL TIP
Reduce the length of big old leaves by half to encourage a greater length of blanched stem.

Harvesting
Dig up the leeks as you need them from September to April. If you want to clear the ground for other crops in spring lift the leeks and just 'heel them in' (covering the roots and stem with soil) using a spare part of the garden. This heeling in also helps extend the period leeks remain fit to eat, as once lifted the plant becomes less quick to

make the second season growth which leads to flowering.

Possible Problems
Should orange dusty spots occur on the leaves, lift plants and destroy leaves (the stem will be edible), ideally by burning. Be sure to rotate crops thereafter to avoid future problems.

Figure 91: Young plants must be watered in at transplanting.

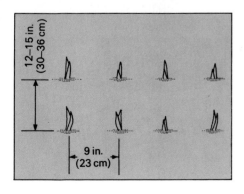

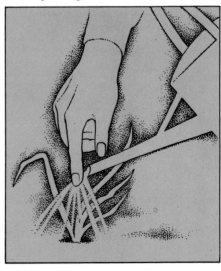

Lettuces

There are four main groups of lettuce (*Lactuca sativa*) varieties – the rounded cabbage types which are further subdivided into soft leaved or butterhead; the curly crisp types; the upright Cos lettuce and finally the open-hearted cut-leaved or oak-leaved types. All require similar cultural conditions although many varieties have specific seasons for sowing and harvesting which are best followed for assured crops.

LETTUCE – CABBAGE BUTTERHEAD

This is by far the most popular of all lettuce in Europe where it is sold all the year round. Its common name of 'Butterhead' perhaps aptly refers to the rich yellowish-green heart it produces, and although it is rather soft-leaved, it is very succulent. This applies particularly to the well-hearted plants harvested in midsummer.

Site and Soil

Any well-cultivated soil is suitable and open sunny sites are best, especially for well-hearted crops raised in the spring and autumn.

Varieties

Hardy and fast-maturing kinds are best for spring and autumn-maturing crops. It is advisable to choose varieties such as 'Avondefiance' which have built-in resistance to disease for the autumn-maturing crops.

Sowing Instructions

Sow indoors in late January/early February and plant out in early March under cloches for the earliest crops. These will be ready to harvest in late May/early June. As soon as soil conditions allow (i.e. the soil is sufficiently dry and free from frost) sow in the cropping site in rows 12 in (30 cm) apart – under cloches and polythene tunnels in March and in the open ground from April onwards.

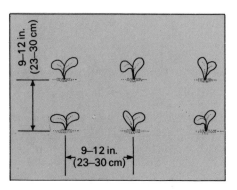

Cabbage Lettuce.

Sow a few seeds every fourteen days from early April to late July/early August so you have a succession of lettuce crops. If early winter conditions are mild, this will give crops from May to December. Sharp frost will shorten the season. Sow hardy types in October under cloches to overwinter and crop in early May.

How to Grow

Prick out your indoor raised seedlings into small pots (peat pots are ideal) before planting out. Thin out the crops sown directly into the ground as soon as they are large enough to handle, spacing them 9–12 in (23–30 cm) apart. Water the plants well in dry weather, giving them an occasional good soaking, rather than repeated light waterings. Give liquid fertiliser in dry weather to speed growth.

Little cultural treatment is needed.

Harvesting

When the weather is warm, crops will be ready to eat within 70 days of sowing. At cooler times of the year they will take up to 90 days. Before cutting to eat, bear down gently on the heart of the lettuce with the back of your hand to test its firmness. Never pinch it as this causes bruising of the heart.

Possible Problems

You can avoid seedling damage in early spring and in wet conditions by using slug bait. Root aphis (lots of greyish greenflies on the roots in midsummer), although a comparatively rare condition, causes plants to be stunted in growth and to wilt. If you use resistant varieties like 'Avondefiance', the likelihood of attack is reduced. This and other varieties are also resistant to mildew – a white mould that affects leaves in autumn and in cold, slow growing conditions.

USEFUL TIP

Compact varieties like Tom Thumb are ideal for the 10 ft × 12 ft (3 m × 4 m) vegetable plot. Space seedlings from 6 in (16 cm) apart.

LETTUCE – CRISP

This group includes the large curly crisp lettuce, particularly popular in USA where they are usually known as the 'Great Lakes' and 'Crisp-head' type. In Britain they are called 'Webb's Wonderful'. Very crisp leaf ribs and hearts are produced by all varieties which stand well in hot weather and, given ideal growing conditions, will grow to a great size.

Site and Soil

Dig all the organic matter you can obtain into the soil to be cropped with lettuce. Well-rotted compost or manure thoroughly mixed with the garden soil retains moisture, and gives the best conditions. As they are shallow-rooted plants it is not necessary to dig the compost deep into the ground. Avoid sites which are heavily shaded by trees overhead and where there is competition from tree roots for moisture. These make it difficult to grow good lettuce.

Figure 92: Lettuce can be grown under cloches through the winter.

Sowing Instructions

Sow in the cropping site in rows 12–15 in (30–37·5 cm) apart every fourteen days or so from March to July. If winter conditions allow (i.e. if frost is not too severe) you can also sow hardy and fast-maturing varieties like 'Windermere' in October to over-winter under cloches, (see figure 92). Alternatively sow them indoors in January/February and plant out in March under polythene. They will be ready to harvest in May.

How to Grow

It is much better in summer to sow small quantities successively than to transplant seedlings. You can thin out seedlings from the sown row and transplant them for early summer maturing crops. This extends the cropping by two to three weeks from one sowing. Thin the seedlings to stand 12 in (30 cm) apart, or a little wider. A wider spacing ensures that largest plants grow in midsummer.

Harvesting

Once the centres start to curl in you can begin to cut the lettuce. As it grows so rapidly start to cut just before the centres are firm and fully developed so you get the longest possible harvest period. As with Cabbage Butterhead test firmness of the heart with the back of your upturned fingers, being careful not to bruise the heart.

Crisp Lettuce.

Possible Problems

Sparrows and other small birds can play havoc at an early stage by eating the leaves of lettuce seedlings. Prevent this by covering the seedlings with polythene tunnel cloches or, for an alternative practical method of protection, push short sticks into the soil along the row and stretch occasional strands of black cotton between them.

The soft brown rot, botrytis, commonly called 'grey mould' because of the soft fluffy grey growth which develops on brown patches can be troublesome in cold, wet conditions. The variety 'Avoncrisp' has resistance to this disease bred into it. It also withstands hot, dry summer conditions.

USEFUL TIP

Salvaged translucent containers, such as are used for milk in America and squashes and bulk detergents in Britain, make good 'cloches' to cover lettuce. Just cut the base off the container, either unscrew and remove the top or cut a small hole in the top for ventilation and put over lettuce. This protects lettuce from birds, as well as cold and wind.

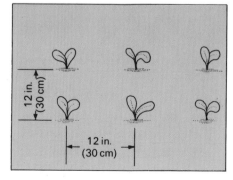

Cos Lettuce.

LETTUCE – COS

Straight upright leaves typify the cos lettuce, which is sometimes called leaf lettuce. The very big-leaved varieties will produce crisp white hearts, and provide an appetising alternative to celery. In my experience these types are not quite as easy to grow as the tightly self-hearting cabbage lettuce, except perhaps for the smaller, somewhat cabbage-lettuce-like types including 'Winter Density' and 'Little Gem'. However the crisp texture and good flavour makes it well worth persevering at growing this type.

Site and Soil

Any open site and any well-cultivated soil is suitable.

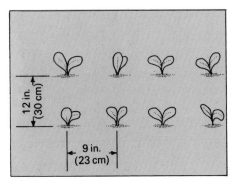

Sowing Instructions

These are the same as instructions for the cabbage lettuce. That is – sow in late January/early February indoors, transplant the seedlings singly into small pots and plant out early spring. Sow in the cropping site at fortnightly intervals from March to June. Make drills ½–1 in. (1–2·5 cm) deep and just cover the seeds with soil. Sow hardy kinds in October under cloches.

How to Grow

Thin and plant out seedlings so they are 9 in (23 cm) apart and with 12 in (30 cm) between the rows. For the 10 ft × 12 ft (3 m × 4 m) vegetable plot compact varieties like 'Little Gem' and 'Winter Density', which can be spaced 6 in (15 cm) and 9 in. (23 cm) respectively between plants and between rows, are particularly suitable.

Very large-leaved kinds like the 'Lobjoits Green Cos' will form the densest blanched hearts if you tie in the outer leaves with raffia or string.

Harvesting

Start to gather the lettuces as soon as the centres begin to develop. By the time you are harvesting the last plants in the row the hearts will be fully developed. If the cutting of any lettuce for eating is delayed particularly in very hot dry weather, plants burst their hearts as the flower head develops. Such plants are then bitter to taste.

Possible Problems

Greenfly can attack lettuce in midsummer and may overwinter. Maintaining hygienic conditions by keeping the plot clear of weeds and old crop remains, which may carry greenfly, helps considerably in avoiding overwintered plant attack. The likelihood of this pest can also be reduced in the summer by keeping the lettuce well watered and thus growing fast. Use sprays based on Resmethrin to knock out greenfly quickly.

The soft brown rot botrytis (see Lettuce – Crisp, Possible Problems) can cause losses, especially on overwintered lettuce. Symptoms of attack occur as the crop is nearing maturity when plants suddenly wilt and go yellow. If you inspect the plant closely you will find a brown mark on the stem at ground level where the plant was infected. Reduce the chances of attack by making sure plants are not set too deep, and the young seedling leaves are not damaged. Also avoid hoe damage to the stem at ground level. Dry, airy atmospheres also reduce attack and you can apply protective fungicide dusts to the plants as well as working it into the surface soil around them.

USEFUL TIP

Never plant lettuce seedlings too deep: this can prevent the formation of hearts. The seedlings should flop over when first transplanted: they soon straighten.

Figure 93: Tie loosely round the outer leaves to improve the hearts.

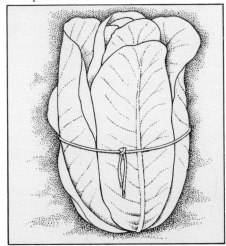

Corn Salad.

LETTUCE – OTHER KINDS

Fringed, curled and cut leaves on open centred plants constitute the majority of varieties under this heading. They include the loose leaved 'Salad Bowl', which produces an abundance of small curled and cut leaves like endive. Another variety – 'Grand Rapids' – is useful to grow under glass to provide winter lettuce leaves for salad, as well as outdoor summer lettuce leaves. The variety 'Continuity' may also be included in this group, although it is actually a butterhead type. However the attractive copper bronzing makes it a novelty.

Celtuce (*Lactuca sativa angustana*) is often described as a mixture of celery and lettuce because the outer leaves are used as lettuce and the heart, including a good proportion of succulent stem, can be used like celery – either cooked or fresh in salads.

'Corn salad' or 'Lamb's lettuce' is another useful open centred lettuce which if sown in August and September will provide lettuce leaves through the winter. Once four or five leaves have formed older leaves can be gathered.

Site and Soil
All garden soils are suitable. Site in similar places to other lettuce types.

Special Siting
While all lettuce may be grown as a crop in its own right or as a quick maturing intercrop between rows of vegetables which take a long time to mature, they are very adaptable plants. Varieties like 'Buttercrunch' and 'Grand Rapids' for example can be grown in window boxes.

The butterhead types grow well in fertilised peat-filled growing bags indoors and on a patio. Compact bright green types like 'Little Gem' and 'Tom Thumb' do not look strangely out of place among flowers and the bronzed 'Continuity' is attractive as well as tasty.

Lettuce 'Continuity'.

Sowing Instructions
Sow all varieties, except 'Corn salad', from April to June in 14 days successional sowings. 'Grand Rapids' can also be sown in the autumn for under-glass cropping in winter. Sow 'Corn Salad' in August and September.

USEFUL TIP
Pull up lettuce, put roots in a jar of water and place in a cool place to extend harvest life in hot weather. Some seedsmen sell packets of mixed varieties of lettuce, which will give the longest possible cropping period from one sowing.

How to Grow
Water well in dry weather and hoe to control weeds. Thin out 'Corn Salad' plants to 3–4 ins (7·5–10 cm) apart, and protect from severe frost with straw and dried grass.

Harvesting
Gather a few leaves at a time from all varieties except 'Continuity' and Celtuce. Cut these like other lettuce.

Possible Problems
None to worry about.

LETTUCE CROPPING CHART

Type/Variety Examples	Sowing Date		Harvesting					
			Jan Feb	Mar Apr	May Jun	Jul Aug	Sept Oct	Nov Dec
Cabbage Butterhead								
Cobham Green ⎫	Sow indoors mid January/February	Plant out under cloches/tunnels			●	● ●		
Suzan	Sow every 14 days in March–May outside					●	● ●	
Sea Queen	Sow under polythene in October				● ●			
Avondefiance	Sow from June to mid August outside	Protect with cloches in early winter to extend crop					● ● ●	●
Kordaat ⎫ Kloek ⎬	Sow and grow in heated greenhouse end September–October				● ● ● ● ● ●			
Cabbage Crisp								
Windermere	Sow outdoors under cloches in October	Sow indoors mid January–February			● ●			
Great Lakes ⎫ Windermere ⎬	Sow outdoors March–mid June					● ● ● ●		
Avoncrisp	Sow outdoors in mid June–mid August	Protect crop in early winter					● ● ● ●	
Cos Winter Density	Sow mid September–October under cloches	Sow outside April–mid July			● ● ●	● ● ●	● ●	●
Lobjoits Green	Sow outside mid March to mid June					● ● ●	●	
One variety from each of the three popular groups will give a year long cropping period –								

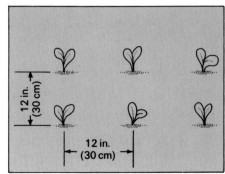

Marrows and Courgettes

One of the earliest and perhaps one of the fastest growing of our garden vegetables is that known as summer squash to Americans, marrow to the British, and when cut very young courgette to the French, *(Cucurbita pepo ovifera)*. In fact in recent years plant breeders have been concentrating on producing prolific new varieties which are particularly ideal for gathering as courgettes, which have thus become well known and popular as a vegetable in Britain too.

Before describing some of these interesting varieties it is as well to cover the cultural details which are common for nearly all types.

Site and Soil

Sunny sites and those with partial shade are suitable although if there is too much shade the leaves will become very large and drawn and cropping will be reduced. An open soil containing plenty of well-rotted compost and manure to retain moisture is the ideal although perfectly adequate crops may be produced in ordinary garden soil.

Green Bush Marrow.

Figure 94: Direct sow marrow seeds on a compost heap. A jam jar acts as a cloche.

These plants will also grow very well planted on the top of well decomposed compost heaps or heaps of rotted down leaves, lawn mowings etc. Perching plants up on the compost heap is a good idea as the large rather sprawling leaves can spread over and smother adjacent crops on small plots. Marrows will grow very fast, but to do so they demand plenty of water. This will be retained by rotted down organic matter. Given this and warm conditions the plants will grow so fast,

you really need to stand well back or become overgrown!

Special Siting

In addition to planting on a compost heap you can also train climbing or trailing varieties along a fence. Alternatively you can put three plants at the points of a triangle and train the stems up a wooden framework to form a

Golden Courgettes.

wigwam shape. In general however the compact bush types are better for the 10 ft × 12 ft (3 m × 4 m) vegetable plot than the trailing kinds.

People who live in flats and homes without gardens can grow courgettes in fertilised peat-filled polythene growing bags placed on a patio, balcony, or outside a back door.

Figure 95: Cross pollination by hand.

Large White Bush Marrow.

Sowing Instructions

Sow seed in 3½ ins (9 cm) pots – two to a pot – in early May. Single out the seedlings as soon as possible and transplant the young plants to the cropping site in early June when there is no more likelihood of frost. Remember, these plants are tender – one frost will kill them and you will have to start again.

An alternative method is to sow

Courgettes (above). An attractive variety of Squash (below).

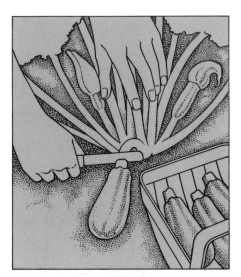

Figure 96: Use an old knife to cut courgettes to avoid damaging plant.

three seeds direct in each cropping site in late May, so they are timed to emerge immediately after any possibility of frost. If you do this it is a good idea to cover the seeds with cloches or polythene tunnels until the seedlings are well established. A simple way to get plants established is to sow two or three seeds under an upturned glass jar which acts as an effective cloche.

How to Grow

Keep the plants very well watered in dry weather and hoe between them to control weeds until the leaves give sufficient canopy to smother any likely weed growth. These plants produce male and female flowers and if you cross-pollinate them by hand, it will increase cropping. To do this, pick a male flower (male flowers have *no* embryo fruit behind the flowers), carefully tear off the petals and gently push the pollen-bearing anthers into several female flowers.

Harvesting

Cut courgettes when the fruits are 4–5 ins (10–12·5 cm) long. Nearly all of the marrow varieties are best harvested while still young. Test them for tenderness by pushing your thumb nail into one rib of the marrow close to the stalk. If your nail slips in easily the marrow is still young enough to cut and eat. You can continue harvesting from late July until the first frost.

The exception to cutting young is the American Winter Squashes which need a long, warm summer to fully mature. When cut, store by hanging in nets in a dry cool place.

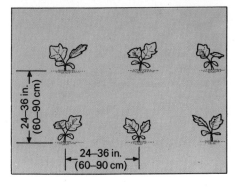

Custard Marrow.

Vegetable Spaghetti.

Two or three well grown plants of most varieties will produce sufficient for the average family of four's needs.

USEFUL TIP

With all marrows, squashes, cucumbers and pumpkins, push the flat seeds pointed end downwards into the soil rather than sowing the flat seeds on their sides. In warm conditions all these seeds germinate in a very few days so don't leave them too long indoors after sowing without checking them.

Possible Problems

Watch out for slugs as the seedlings develop and put down slug bait if necessary. Plants may also be attacked occasionally by mosaic virus, which stunts the growth, and makes the leaves mottled yellow and puckered. It is best to destroy plants thus affected, so remember to sow one or two extra plants to be on the safe side.

If your plants are suffering from lack of moisture, they are likely to get mildew in the form of a greyish mould on their leaves. Providing this is not too severe, it should not affect the crop's growth or flavour.

Varieties

Courgettes. Varieties are now available which have been especially bred to produce masses of small fruits 3–5 in (7·5–12·5 cm) long over an extended period. They include smooth, rich green skinned fruits; mottled cream and green fruits and the rich golden yellow of varieties like 'Golden Zucchini'. If the fruits are left on these plants they will develop further to give

Figure 97: Marrows growing up a tripod.

'marrow' fruits 12 ins (30 cm) or so long. These may either be stuffed and baked or cooked separately.

Marrows: the best known types in Britain are either the Bush or Trailing Marrow varieties. Several fruits, 12–24 ins (30–60 cm) long are produced on each plant and they can be creamy white, green or striped in colour. The varieties known as 'Long Green Trailing' and 'Long White Trailing' produce plants which will cover an area more than 6 ft square (0·5 square metres) and carry very large marrows. These fruits can be cut and stored for a short time like Winter Squashes (see under Harvesting). These varieties, however, are not very suitable for the 10 ft × 12 ft (3 m × 4 m) vegetable plot – a compact F₁ hybrid like 'Green Bush' would be better. Some of the early fruit produced can be picked as courgettes, while a few others can be left to grow into marrows 12 ins (30 cm) and longer.

A little more bizarre are the Custard Marrow, the fruits of which look rather like space age 'flying saucers' with scalloped edges. There are both white and yellow-skinned varieties, and they should be cut and cooked young for the best flavour.

Finally there is the squash 'Vegetable Spaghetti', which is ready for the first harvesting in 65 days from sowing, providing it has had warm growing conditions. The fruits should be cut when they are 8 ins (20 cm) or so long. To cook them place in boiling water for 20–30 minutes. Cut open the squash, remove the spaghetti-like centre, season it with salt and pepper before eating.

Melons

In the past, growing melons (*Cucumis melo*) has been very much the province of the skilled gardener who was able to produce a humid, tropical atmosphere in a glasshouse. Nowadays, the new varieties, including F₁ hybrids like 'Sweetheart', are much easier to grow and give very worthwhile crops in home garden conditions. They need warm positions, warm summer and ample moisture, but the results are well worth everyone having a try.

Site and Soil

All varieties will grow well in glasshouses, but you can also grow the Cantaloupe types in frames, under cloches and, in very warm areas, against south-facing walls. Give them masses of well-rotted organic matter which encourages extensive root development and helps to provide ample moisture. Planting melons on well-rotted down compost heaps is a good idea, or alternatively dig plenty of manure and compost into the soil.

Sowing Instructions

Sow seeds either singly in pots, or put two seeds to a pot, but reduce to one as

> **USEFUL TIP**
>
> Fresh cut melons can be cubed and kept in the deep freeze to give succulent fruit the whole year round.

soon as the seedlings are under way. The best time for sowing is in late April/early May. Sow earlier only if you have access to a heated greenhouse. Although a good long growing season is required, it is better to delay

Cantaloupe Melon.

Figure 98: Support melons as they grow to keep them free from dirt splashes.

sowing rather than to expose the young plants to low temperatures. Ideal temperatures are 70°F (21°C) for germinating the seed and 55–60°F (13°–15°C) for further growing.

How to Grow

In greenhouses train the plants up a wire as described for cucumbers. Out in the open, put two plants in an area 4 ft × 6 ft (120 × 180 cm) and 'hill' up the soil a little to plant on a mound. Avoid water resting around the stem.

Once the main stem has produced five large leaves, pinch out the growing tip (see cucumbers). Pinch out subsequent side-shoots at the growing tip when three leaves have developed. Unless you pinch out these growing tips the frame will become filled with leafy growth and the plants will produce few or no fruits.

Melons, like marrows, will need cross-pollination. If you are doing this by hand, the best time is at midday when the pollen is dry and fluffy.

When the plants are growing strongly keep them well watered, and give them liquid feed as the first young fruits reach the size of a walnut. Reduce feeding and watering when the fruits begin to reach harvesting size. As they get larger, gently lift the fruits and rest them on a piece of board to keep them clean.

Harvesting

Test for ripeness by pressing the end furthest from the stalk with your thumb. If the fruit 'gives' a little it will be ripe. Brown, corky cracking on the fruit and a sweet, delicious smell also indicate that the fruit is ripe.

Melons growing

Possible Problems

Plants may be subject to attack from red spider mites which can be avoided by keeping the growing atmosphere really damp (spraying the foliage regularly with water helps to achieve this). In hot dry conditions red spiders multiply quickly. They turn the leaves bronzy-brown and check plant growth.

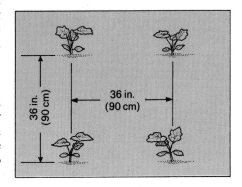

Mustard, Cress and Watercress

Mustard and cress (*Sinapis alba* and *Lepidium sativum*) are the simplest salad ingredients to grow, and are an increasingly popular garnish to all kinds of cooked dishes. There are two kinds of cress, the curled – which may give a little more bulk – and the plain-leaved type. Mustard is very often replaced nowadays by rape (*Brassica rapus*) for commercial crops.

Watercress (*Nasturtium officinale*) can be grown in garden soil, or under cold glass in border soil as long as the soil is kept constantly moist. However, a stream or running water is really needed if it is to crop repeatedly over a number of years from one planting. Obviously neither of these crops are suitable for inclusion in the 10 ft × 12 ft (3 × 4 m) vegetable plot.

MUSTARD AND CRESS
Sowing Instructions
You can sow the seeds at any time of the year. In a temperature of about 50°F (10°C), allow two to three weeks between sowing and harvesting. If you want to grow mustard and cress so

Watercress.

they are ready at the same time, sow the cress four days before the mustard. Sow a small quantity every fourteen days to obtain a succession of harvestable foliage.

How to Grow
All you need is a saucer covered with two or three dampened paper tissues, a piece of kitchen paper towel or blotting paper on which you scatter the seeds. An alternative growing method is to fill a shallow plastic tray ¼–1 in (1–2 cm) deep with peat or seedling

Mustard and Cress.

compost. Sprinkle the cress seed over this; keep it damp and in the dark for three days and then sprinkle the mustard seed on top, or grow the two separately if you prefer. Once the seed leaves start to unfold immediately move the tray to the light, by placing it on a window sill. Leave it there until you cut the crop for eating. The main advantage of growing cress in peat is that the brown seed cases are more likely to be left behind at harvesting stage, thus saving you the trouble of washing them off when preparing for eating.

Harvesting
Cut off at the base of the stem when the plants are 2 in (5 cm) or so high. You can slice them off with a sharp knife but the easier method is to take a handful of tops in the fingers of one hand and cut off a bundle of stems using scissors.

Problems
There are none.

Notes
Mustard and cress can also be sown and grown outside but is much easier to cut and clean if it has been grown indoors. The usual outdoor sowing at ½ lb (225 gms) of mustard seed to 50 sq yd (41·8 sq m) is to provide a green manure crop. The plants produce masses of foliage very quickly, especially in the summer, which is then dug back into the soil to provide organic matter. It helps to put some nitrogenous fertiliser down at the time of digging which speeds the rotting down and avoids a shortage of nitrogen if a crop is sown too quickly following the green manure crop.

WATERCRESS
Site and Soil
Fresh water in a running stream is the ideal site. Check with your local water authority to see the water is free of health hazards before planting.

Sowing Instructions
Raise young plants from seed sown in boxes indoors, then prick off seedlings into more boxes to produce plants 3–4 in (7·5–10 cm) high to plant in streams and the garden. You can also sow direct in the garden soil in April. When the plants have 4 in (10 cm) long shoots they can be planted in streams, 4–6 in (10–15 cm) apart.

How to Grow
Once planted the only treatment is to make sure they have plenty of water. Trimming over the plants late summer removes straggly growth and flowering shoots. If you are not growing in a stream, dig a shallow trench and add compost to the base. Once planted, keep very well watered.

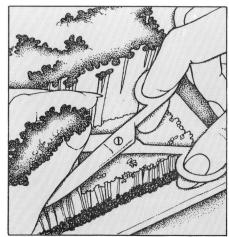

Figure 99: Cutting Cress.

Harvesting
Cutting can begin in the autumn on beds planted in the spring.

Possible Problems
None to worry about.

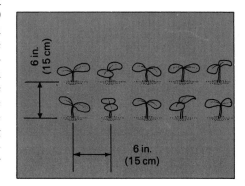

Okra

The slender green seed pods of okra (*Hibiscus esculentus*) are delicious for flavouring soups and stews. They may also be cooked and served on their own as a vegetable. Given treatment and conditions similar to those for outdoor tomatoes, okra is easy to grow, but it is currently only stocked by a few specialists, and thus is not very easy to obtain. Its common name 'Lady's Fingers' aptly describes the shape of the fruit, the garden varieties of which are clearly ridged but do not have the masses of small spines that are sometimes found on those for sale in greengrocers.

Site and Soil
A warm sheltered site is essential in cold areas and a southerly facing plot, against a fence or wall is best. All reasonably well cultivated soils are suitable, but light, sandy soils improved by the addition of well-rotted compost to help water retention are the ideal. Warm situations and good soils will produce vigorously growing plants 4 ft (120 cm) high.

USEFUL TIP
Like various other vegetables – aubergines and tomatoes for example – Okra grown in peat bags make attractive as well as productive plants for patios, balconies or terraces.

Okra growing, showing the yellow flowers.

Sowing Instructions
Sow indoors in early May and then plant outside once there is no more possibility of frost. Alternatively sow direct in the cropping site under cloches or polythene tunnels in

Okra seed pods shown gathered ready for cooking.

mid-May. A single row is ample for the ordinary family's needs.

How to Grow
Thin out the seedlings and space plants 20–24 ins (50–60 cm) apart. Hoe between the plants occasionally to control weeds. Water well in dry weather and give liquid fertiliser every

Figure 100: Okra growing in a fertilised peat-filled bag.

fourteen days or so from the time the first yellow flowers open.

Harvesting
Once the fruits are 6–8 ins (15–20 cm) long you can begin harvesting. Plants raised from a May sowing are likely to be ready to start picking in mid to late August. If you pick the fruit regularly, not only do you have a constant supply of succulent pods, but the plants will continue to fruit up to the first frost.

Possible Problems
There are none to worry about. Very strong growing plants may need a cane or stake to stop them blowing over.

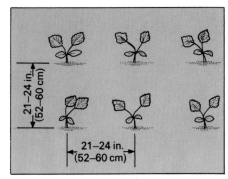

21–24 in. (52–60 cm)

21–24 in. (52–60 cm)

Onions and Shallots

To grow massively big onions (*Allium cepa*) fit for exhibition at vegetable shows from seed is quite a test for the gardener's skill, but to grow onions, either to use green for salads or as bulbs for pickling and cooking, is very easy. The challenge and difficulty of growing the giants has perhaps been given too much publicity, so it has tended to mask the ease of cultivating onions for culinary purposes.

ONIONS FOR SALADS

All varieties of onions may be sown to pull young as salad onions, but if you want them specifically for this purpose the special varieties like 'White Lisbon' are best. Good alternatives are the silver-skinned varieties like 'Paris Silver-Skin' (which really is a silver colour in comparison to the white of 'White Lisbon'), or 'Cocktail'. If you leave some onions from these two cultivars in the row after pulling those you want for salads, they will grow into 'mouth-sized' onions.

Site and Soil

Any cultivated soil is suitable and they will grow in pretty well any site in the

Spring Onions just starting to bowl.

Spring Onions pulled very young

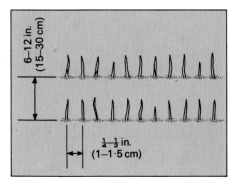

garden. If you want neat tight bulbs for pickling choose a more open sunny site than those for salad purposes.

Sowing Instructions

Sow the seed in very shallow drills and just cover with soil. Rows can be as close as 6 in (15 cm) although a 12 in (30 cm) spacing will make inter-row hoeing easier. Sow once a month from March to September to give salad onions the year round – (the September batch will provide them through the winter). The best crops of bulbs for pickling will be those you gather twelve to sixteen weeks after the March/April sowings.

How to Grow

Hoe between the rows occasionally to control the weeds. The thin grassy leaves of the sowings may take a little time to show and it helps to mix a little fast-germinating radish seed in with the onions. This acts as a guide when you hoe to destroy weeds early in the year, and also gives you an indication of where the onions will follow. Grow spring onions sown in September/October under cold glass and polythene, and you will get a very good winter salad crop. This applies even in cold districts.

Harvesting

Pull the green onions as soon as they are large enough to eat, taking the largest first and leaving the smaller ones to grow some more. Lift small bulb onions for pickling when the bulbs have reached pickling size and then leave them to ripen in the sun. Onions which are green when lifted will shrink back as they dry.

Possible Problems

Plants may be affected by the disease white rot, which causes yellowing of the leaves and white fluffy mould at the base of the bulb. To prevent the build-up of this disease in the soil it is essential to follow a strict rotation plan, in which you avoid cropping the same land with onions year after year. As another cultural aid, avoid sowing too thickly. Once in the soil white rot will persist for years. If you have to use soil which has been proved to contain it, sprinkle 4% calomel dust down the row in with the seed, at the rate of 1 oz to 15 yd (5 gm to 3 metres).

Small maggots attacking the roots are likely to be the larvae of onion fly, a pest which is most prevalent on dry, light soils. Lift and burn any infected plants and treat the seed rows with chemicals such as diazinon granules.

ONIONS FROM SEEDS

The cheapest way to make sure you have a continuous supply of cooking onions to bake, boil, fry or use raw is to raise them from seed. Given reasonably fine, crumbly soil at sowing time they are quite easy to grow. There is a choice of shape – either globe onions or flat-bottomed bulbs. The slightly milder-flavoured scarlet-bulbed onions are attractive for use raw.

Site and Soil

A well-cultivated garden soil and an open sunny site are the requirements: the better the soil the bigger the onions are likely to grow.

Sowing Instructions

There are three possible sowing dates. The first and by far the most popular is in spring. In practice this varies from late February to early April, the right time being when you can rake down and firm the soil and draw out a very shallow drill. Once again, the earlier the onions are sown and established the larger they are likely to be. You can lift bulbs from this sowing in early autumn to store and use through the winter and following spring.

Mid-August is the next sowing time, but for this you must choose the 'overwintering varieties'. These come from places as far apart as Switzerland and Japan and have names like 'Express', 'Presto', 'Imai' and 'Senshyu'. These varieties produce sturdy plants by the winter and the bulbs are ready to pull in June and early July.

You can also sow ordinary bulb onion varieties out of doors in late September to overwinter on the cropping site. This provides the longest

Globe Onion.

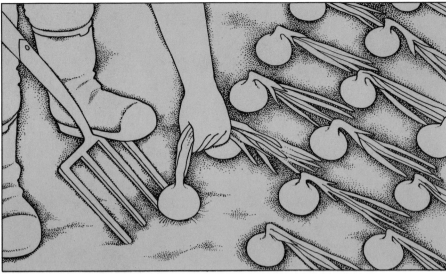

Figure 101: Ease onions gently out of the ground before drying in the sun.

growing season, and gives big bulbs, but the overwintering losses can be quite high. The more acceptable winter sowing for big and exhibition bulbs is to sow indoors from December to early February, growing the young seedlings under cold glass and planting them out on the cropping site in March.

A March/April sowing and possibly also a September one to provide winter salads, will probably give the 'casual gardener' the least worry!

How to Grow

Once seedlings are showing and established, the onions need spacing to 4–5 in (10–12.5 cm) apart. Thin them first however to 2 in (5 cm) and then thin again about a month later to 4 in (10 cm). This ensures you have a full row of plants and also provides a succession of salad onions from the thinnings. Gaps can be filled by transplanting thinned out plants. Space the rows 9–12 in (23–30 cm) apart, so there are six to eight plants per square foot (900 sq cm). to give maximum yield.

Harvesting

When the plants are fully grown, bend over the tops to prevent further flow of sap. After a week or two lift the onions by easing them out of the soil after loosening with a fork, and put them base up in the sun to ripen off completely. Then either tie them to a rope to hang up – Brittany onion-sellers' style, or place them in trays. Store them in a dry, airy, cool but frost-free place. If they do get frosted be especially careful to avoid knocking or bruising them as in this condition rot spots will quickly develop.

Red Onion.

Possible Problems

Swollen, distorted and bloated leaves are symptoms of attack by eelworm – tiny creatures which are not easily seen with the naked eye. Avoid growing onions for at least two years on land which has been shown to contain this pest. Modern seed treatments should reduce the chance of this pest occurring at any stage.

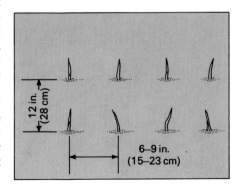

Onions and Onion sets.

ONIONS FROM SETS

There really is no easier crop to grow than onions from sets. Just push these small bulbs into cultivated soil from February to April, hoe occasionally to control weeds and then harvest the bulbs. This method of growing is especially valuable in colder climates where short growing seasons and wet conditions are not favourable for seed-raised bulb crops.

Site and Soil

As for seed-raised onions.

Planting

Trim the wispy strawy piece on the top of the set either with scissors or by pinching off with your fingers. If you leave these the birds will pull the sets up by this wispy piece and the worms will pull the bulb into the ground. In fact this does no more than misplace the set in the row, but if you remove

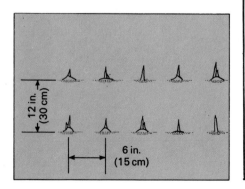

the wispy piece, there is no future need to replant pulled-out sets.

To plant, either draw out a very shallow drill, space the bulbs along it and cover with soil, or push them very gently into the soil until they are just covered. Space the bulbs 6 in (15 cm) apart and the rows 9–12 in (23–30 cm) apart. A ½ lb (0.2 kg) of average size sets plants a 30–45 ft (9–13.5 m) long row.

How to Grow/Harvesting

The procedure for these is the same as that for bulb onions from seed. Lift onions from sets once the leaves turn yellow and start to ripen. If you leave them in the soil and a heavy rainfall follows dry sunny weather, there is the chance of the onion starting to grow again and the base of the bulb splitting as a result.

USEFUL TIP

If some of your onions form a flower bud prematurely (known as 'bolting') rather than developing a good bulb, break out the bud as soon as it appears. Use these poorer onions first. You can avoid bolting in seed-grown onions by sowing the seed a week or two later, and in onion sets by selecting and planting smaller sizes of sets. Smaller onion sets are not only less likely to run to seed but also give you more for your money as you are buying by weight.

SHALLOTS

Shallots are much larger than onion sets, but they require exactly the same treatment. Very easy to grow, they store longer than many crops of onions and to the gourmet are the perfect seasoning for many dishes. Each planted shallot will grow and multiply to produce four to eight new shallots.

Siting, Planting and Growing

All exactly the same as for onion sets.

Harvesting

Lift once the leaves have yellowed and are beginning to die down. When the shallots are really dry and fully ripened, tie them in bundles or store them in trays. Select a few of the smaller shallots (1 in (2 cm) diameter) of good shape and keep these for the next year's planting.

Possible Problems

All bulb onions are open to attack by neck rot, a soft brown rot which starts

Shallots.

at the stem in store and quickly spreads through the onion. Reduce the likelihood of attack by treating seed and spraying crops in June with fungicide like Benomyl.

Note

The 'Welsh Onion', *Allium fistulosum*, raised from spring-sown seed, is a perennial plant producing green leek-like shoots which can be pulled to use either green for salads ro cooked for flavouring all the year round. Established plants need lifting, dividing up and replanting every second or third year, spacing them as for shallots.

Parsnips

The parsnip (*Pastinaca sativa*) is one of the hardiest of root vegetables and actually improves in flavour after exposure to frost. Although this vegetable is one of the earliest to be sown in spring and produces larger roots with the longest growing season, the current tendency is to grow smaller roots which some people find easier to cope with in the kitchen.

Site and Soil
Avoid heavily overshadowed sites. All ordinary garden soils will produce worthwhile crops, but those which have been well dug in the autumn and have had rotted organic matter added for previous crops are the best.

Sowing Instructions
Sow seed any time from late February to April, when the soil surface is reasonably dry and crumbly. Space the rows 12–15 in (30–38 cm) apart and choose a calm day for sowing, otherwise the large flat seeds blow everywhere! Always use new seed as the germination life is short, (see chart, page 21).

How to Grow
Thin the seedlings in two stages, firstly to 2–3 in (5–7·5 cm) apart and then, when these are well established, to the final spacing distance of 4–6 in (10–15 cm). If you want large roots (which are in fact the quickest to peel and give a more edible vegetable) space the rows 15–18 in (38–45 cm) apart and grow two plants per square foot (900 sq cm) of garden. For smaller roots of a similar size to those purchased prepacked in supermarkets (rather like big carrots), grow four per 12 in (30 cm) row, and use one of the smaller-rooted varieties such as 'Avonresister'. The smaller foliage of

Parsnips.

Figure 102: Thin seedlings in two stages.

this variety also makes it ideal for the 10 ft × 12 ft (3 m × 4 m) vegetable plot.

Parsnips need little cultural treatment, except for hoeing between rows and plants to control weeds.

USEFUL TIP
Lift a few roots in early autumn and leave on the surface of the soil to get the full benefit of the first 'flavour-improving' frosts.

Harvesting
Dig up the roots as you require them. Parsnips can be left in the ground throughout the winter, but as it is difficult to get them out of solidly frozen soil, lift some earlier and store them for your winter supply. You should certainly lift the remaining roots in early spring and store them in peat or sand, otherwise they will start to grow again. This spoils the roots.

Possible Problems
None to worry about. The rusty brown marks, usually close to the shoulders of a root, are caused by the disease canker. Use resistant varieties like 'Avonresister' to reduce this damage, but in fact it just needs peeling off when the roots are prepared for cooking and eating.

Attacks by maggots of carrot fly sometimes precede canker, and you can control this by applying bromophos granules to the soil.

Plants producing several twisted roots are difficult to prepare for eating. Avoid sowing in freshly manured soil, to reduce the chance of producing these awkwardly forked or multi-rooted specimens.

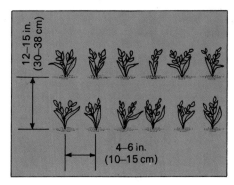

Peas

Second only to salads is the growing of garden peas (*Pisum sativum*) as a must for the small home vegetable garden. Young peas picked fresh from the garden and cooked with a flavouring of mint in early summer are a delicacy which, for me, surpass the more exotic flavour of asparagus or globe artichokes.

The early and late sown pea crops are usually the most successful for everyone and certainly for gardeners who have to contend with hot dry summers. The round-seeded varieties are the most hardy and resistant to cold wet soil conditions but the very wrinkled and somewhat larger-seeded varieties are heavier yielding and better quality, especially when picked a few days past the very young succulent pea stage.

Varieties

Seed catalogues usually list peas under the three headings: 'First Early', 'Second Early' and 'Maincrop' or 'Late'. These headings indicate the period of time from sowing to harvest, which for an early sowing of the 'First Early' types is within 80–85 days, and up to 100 days for 'Late' types. Hot weather will give premature and lighter crops. Varieties from the three groups can be selected to give a succession of crops, but as well as variety, the weather is an important factor. Commercial growers dedicated to keeping the harvesting machines and freezer factories working steadily throughout the cropping period keep a careful watch on the temperature after sowing. If the weather is warm, growth will be rapid and sowing once every fourteen days will provide successional crops. If the weather is cold after sowing, growth will be slower, so the period between sowings will have to be extended.

Site and Soil

All garden sites and soils will produce acceptable crops. In my experience, soil that is cultivated for the first time in a number of years will produce very good crops, be it old grass left undisturbed for a long time or a mixture of top and sub-soil left by builders on a new house site. It is worthwhile remembering that peas will take nitrogen from the air and convert it to nitrogenous plant food, leaving the soil richer than before. A slightly alkaline soil will encourage the activity of bacteria which work with pea roots to convert the nitrogen, so add a dust-

Maincrop Peas.

Figure 103: *Various ways of supporting peas as they grow.*

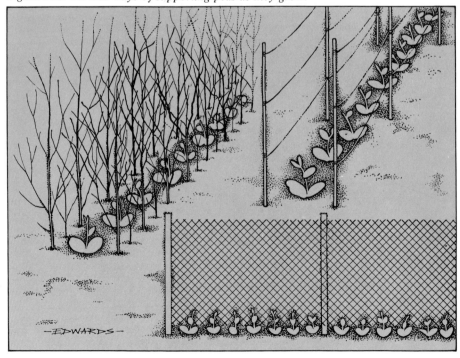

ing of lime or chalk to acid soils. Round pin-head sized globules on the roots of all peas and beans denote the presence of bacteria.

You can increase the growth of peas and thus get a larger crop, by adding organic matter to the soil. This will hold moisture, so is particularly valuable in the event of hot dry weather.

Sowing Instructions

For the earliest crops, sow directly into the cropping site, either in late October/early November (in sheltered areas and under cloches) or in early March. Crops from this sowing will be ready for picking in late May/early June. You can also sow in pots indoors in late January/early February, planting them out under cloches in March to get an early crop. After these sowings, sow successively in the cropping site through the spring and into early summer (see chart for more details).

Sow seeds in a V-shaped drill 2–3 in

tection against the weather and birds. When the seedlings are 2–3 in (5–7·5 cm) high they will need some form of support. For the simplest and minimum form of support, push a few sticks or canes into the soil on either side of the row, and tie horizontal strings between them at 6–12 in (15–30 cm) intervals from the ground. A better alternative is to fix plastic or wire netting up one or both sides of the row. The netting can be used for a number of years. Personally, however, I prefer to erect twigs like a neat fence on each side of the row, with the tops of the sticks trimmed off in a line to the height stated for each variety.

After providing some form of support, no other cultural treatment is needed apart from occasional hoeing to control weeds. In dry weather and where slow growth occurs you can improve crops by spraying with a foliar fertiliser. Plants take this in through their leaves and it is known as a foliar feed.

Late crop Peas.

You may find small maggots, which are the larvae of the pea moth in the pods when you are shelling the peas. These moths are most active in June/July, when they lay their eggs in the flowers. The larvae then hatch and develop in the pods. You can control them by spraying the plants at flowering time, but do this in the evening to reduce the chance of harming bees. The easiest method of control is to grow early and late crops which do not flower in the June/July egg-laying period.

Sowing in cold soil may result in seedling losses and you can reduce this by using round-seeded varieties. It is advisable to use a fungicidal seed dressing as well. Sow a few extra seeds at the end of the row to provide some extra plants to transplant in gaps, should they occur.

PEAS – less common types
There are three main types of pea other than the best known garden varieties. Firstly, the very small, neat and round 'Petit Pois', so popular on the continent of Europe, especially in France. The gourmet will tell you

Pea Cropping Chart

Type/Variety	Sowing Date	Harvesting					
		May	Jun	Jul	Aug	Sept	Oct
First Early e.g. Feltham First	Outdoors Oct/Nov Indoors Jan/Feb Outdoors March	●	● ● ●				
Second Early e.g. Early Onward	March/April			● ● ●			
Maincrop e.g. Lord Chancellor	April			● ● ●	● ● ●		
First Early	mid June					● ● ●	● ● ●

(5–7·5 cm) deep, spacing them to give 11 plants per square foot (900 sq cm). Sow dwarf varieties to give 16 plants per 12 in (30 cm) of row, spacing the rows 15–18 in (38–45 cm) apart, i.e. the same distance as the likely height of the plants. Seed packets and catalogues will give the approximate height for each variety, some of which grow to 5–6 ft (approximately 2 m). The richer the soil the taller the peas are likely to grow, so it is advisable to choose the dwarf varieties for the 10 ft × 12 ft (3 m × 4 m) vegetable plot!

How to Grow
It is a good idea to cover the young seedlings of early crops with polythene tunnels or cloches as pro-

Harvesting
As soon as the peas in the pods are large enough to eat, gather them by holding the stalk in one hand and pulling the pods off with the other. Pick over the row several times, taking the plumpest pods first. Peas are ideal for deep freezing but they must be gathered before the pods start to wrinkle up near the stem. If you leave them to reach this stage, the peas will be old, mealy and starchy.

Possible Problems
Watch out for mice which eat the newly sown seeds in the winter months. To guard against such attack, it is advisable to put down mouse bait or traps immediately after sowing.

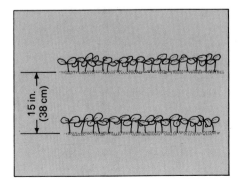

Sugar Peas.

Mange Tout.

these peas need to be steamed in the pod and then shelled ready for eating to retain the full flavour. They are actually very similar to the ordinary peas which have been picked and cooked very young.

Secondly, there is the 'Mange Tout', commonly called 'Sugar Pea' which is not only cooked in the pod, but both pod and peas are then eaten. As the name indicates, 'Mange Tout', you eat everything! Ideal for busy cooks with no time to shell the ordinary kinds, these must be gathered while still young. If allowed to age, the pods become stringy.

The third type, the 'Asparagus Pea', is possibly more unusual and, as indicated by its Latin name *Lotus tetragonolobus*, it is not a true pea but more of a vetch. It has clover-shaped leaves, grows 18 in–2 ft (45–60 cm) in height and spread, and has reddish-purple, attractive flowers. The pods are winged or perhaps better described as 'deeply grooved' and they are cooked whole like 'Mange Tout'.

'Petit Pois' and 'Mange Tout' are grown in exactly the same way as the better known pea varieties, so follow cultural instructions given on the previous pages. The following instructions are for the 'Asparagus Pea' which needs different treatment.

Site and Soil
The same as for the better known varieties of peas.

Sowing Instructions
Sow indoors in late March/early April and set out plants in the cropping position 18 in (45 cm) apart in mid-May. You can also sow directly into the ground from April to June.

USEFUL TIPS

1. 'Recette' peas are an interesting variety which have triple pods.
2. If a row of ordinary peas produces more pods than you can gather to either eat fresh or freeze for future use, they can be left on the plant and allowed to ripen to provide seed for next year. Alternatively, such seeds can be used as a vegetable after soaking in water for 24 hours, but select the green seeded varieties for this.

How to Grow
Keep the soil moist at all times to give the longer cropping period. Providing you do this and the weather is warm, you can gather pods regularly from mid-June up until the frost. No other cultural treatment is required, except occasional hoeing to control weeds in

Asparagus Peas.

the early stage of growth. These plants do not need staking, and in fact they will soon cover the ground, so smothering any weeds.

Harvesting
Gather the young pods when they are 1–2 in (2·5–5 cm) long. At this young stage they have lots of flavour, but if you leave them you will find the resulting older pods rather tough and full of fibre. Cook the pods by steaming them whole with butter for five minutes or so and then eat them rather like asparagus tips.

Peppers and Chillies

There is a distinct difference between the sweet pepper, *Capiscum annuum*, and the very hot chilli or cayenne pepper, *Capiscum frutescens*. The fruits of the sweet pepper are large and rather square lobed and they may be cooked as a vegetable or used fresh in salads. The much smaller, more pointed fruits of the cayenne pepper are used fresh for flavouring or they may be dried and ground up to provide chilli powder. They are perhaps more tender than sweet peppers in their growing state and slightly warmer conditions. For assured results, it is best to grow cayenne peppers under cover.

There are not, as is often believed red and green varieties of sweet pepper. They all start off green, like tomatoes, and turn red as they ripen. If you want the maximum yield from each plant it is advisable to gather the sweet peppers while they are still green. If left on the plant until they turn red, the total number of fruits yielded by the plant is reduced.

The pepper may appear to be a very exotic vegetable to have growing in your garden, but it is just as easy to grow as the tomato and requires very similar treatment.

Sweet Pepper.

Varieties

The recently introduced F₁ hybrid varieties of sweet pepper are both earlier and heavier yielding and are preferable to other varieties. This is especially so in the case of plants to be cropped outside. Hot peppers have very much smaller leaves, and are more branched. As the fruits are smaller – usually long, thin and tapering – they are much lighter cropping.

Site and Soil

For the best results and heaviest crops, grow peppers in a glasshouse or polythene structure. Sweet peppers are in fact excellent plants for polythene houses. You can also raise plants indoors and plant them out in warm districts in warm and sheltered spots, such as against south facing walls and fences. A sunny site is certainly essential to provide the warmth they need.

All well-cultivated garden soils will give reasonable results, but those containing plenty of organic matter will give the heaviest yields as they encourage root development.

Special Siting

In addition to the greenhouse and sunny spots, peppers are attractive plants to grow in large pots on patios, terraces and balconies. They are even worth a try in window boxes, and although the severe root restriction will have the effect of producing small fruit, they are nevertheless quite usable. As they are very similar to tomatoes, peppers will also grow well in the polythene growing bags filled with fertiliser-enriched peat. These bags can be used in greenhouses, and on patios and terraces instead of pots.

I have explained the necessity to rotate crops in order to avoid exhausting specific plant foods and encouraging the build-up of disease in the soil. This is particularly applicable to growing edible crops in greenhouse border soil. The sweet pepper provides a very good alternative to tomato and cucumber to give a three-year crop rotation under glass.

Sowing Instructions

Sow the seeds of all peppers from mid-March to early May. The later sowing is recommended for plants to

Ripe and green peppers. The fruits may be harvested at either stage.

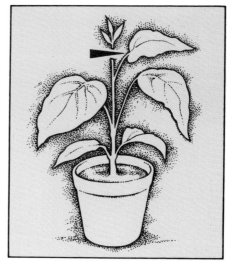

Figure 104: Pinch out growing tips on young plants.

Cayenne Peppers.

tomato fertiliser so as to improve the ultimate weight of crop.

Harvesting
As soon as the fruits are large enough, cut them off at the stem with a sharp knife or secateurs. One plant per person should provide enough for the average family, and both sweet and hot peppers are gathered green for general cooking purposes. If you want good large sweet peppers (perhaps for example to cut in half, remove the seeds from the centre and stuff before baking), and if you are not quite sure when they have reached full size, leave one or two fruits on the plant until they start to turn red. At this point you will see just how large they are likely to get. Keep gathering the fruit once a week – remember the more you gather the greater the weight of peppers each plant will produce. Mid-March raised plants put out under polythene houses in early May will crop from mid-June to early November given average to warm temperatures.

Possible Problems
None to worry about. Just keep a watch out for greenfly and spray with suitable insecticide if they do arrive. Attack by Red Spider Mites in hot dry weather can be controlled by syringing the plants with water.

be grown outdoors in colder districts. It is better to sow later than to risk the chance of checking the plants' growth by keeping them indoors in small pots, while you wait for frost-free planting conditions. Prick off the seedlings into 3½ in (9 cm) pots of potting compost as soon as they are large enough to handle, but continue to grow them in a light position until they are 6 in (15 cm) or more high. A temperature of 55–60°F (13–15°C) is necessary to raise these plants indoors.

How to Grow
Pinch out the central growing point of the young pot plants when they are 6 in (15 cm) high. This produces a bushy, well-branched plant and improves cropping. After this either transplant the plants into larger (8–10 in (20–25 cm) diameter) pots, or plant them 18 in (45 cm) apart in the cropping site. Growth is quite strong, so under glass and in a warm position, you will need to provide a stake or cane to support the plants. Remember they can reach a height of 4 ft (120 cm).

Syringe the plants with water in hot dry weather to help the flowers set fruit. Give them doses of liquid feed every seven to ten days when the first fruits start to swell. It helps to give heavier crops. If you have to delay transplanting from the 3½ in (9 cm) pots for any reason, water the plants every five to seven days with a liquid

Decorative 'Christmas' Chillies.

USEFUL TIPS
1. Try growing one or two hot peppers in flower pots on the window sill. While restricting the roots will reduce the crop, you will only want small quantities of this vegetable for flavouring and the pot plants should provide enough for the average family. If left to turn from green to red the fruits will provide an attractive display.
2. If growing plants in pots, allow a few flowers to set before pinching out the central growing point to get very early fruits.

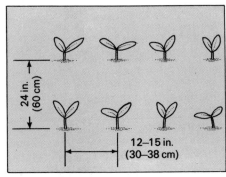

24 in. (60 cm)

12–15 in. (30–38 cm)

Potatoes

New potatoes (*Solanum tuberosum*) lifted fresh from the garden are – like tender young peas – a real early summer delicacy. It is possible that growing maincrop potatoes will take up too much space for their ultimate crop value in the average home garden, but every garden, no matter how small, should be able to accommodate a few potato plants to supply those delectable early new potatoes. You should certainly have a few potatoes growing in the 10 ft × 12 ft (3 × 4 m) vegetable plot. Quite apart from the flavour, having a few potatoes which can be lifted from the garden whenever you want them guards against the inevitability of running out of those you have purchased, which always happens at the most inconvenient time! In addition, really freshly-lifted potatoes are much easier to scrape than those which have been lifted for a while, thus giving the skins time to 'set'.

Site and Soil

All gardens are suitable although crops will be light if grown in heavily-shaded spots or where the soil is very light. You will get the heaviest yields from well-cultivated soil with plenty of well-rotted organic matter dug into it. You can clean up garden soil infested with weeds considerably by planting potatoes. The strong foliage smothers growing weeds and the earthing-up cultural treatment checks the weed root growth. Potatoes are therefore a good crop for a new piece of land which has just been dug, in preparation for vegetable cropping. They are also useful to clean land in a new garden before planting lawns, perennial flowers and shrubs.

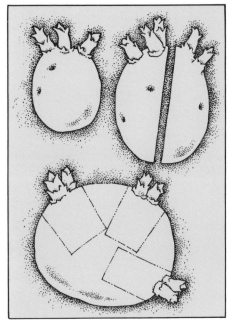

Figure 105: Cut seed potatoes to make planting pieces.

Planting

'Seed potatoes' are not seeds as such, but tubers from the previous year's crop. Ideally they should be about 2–3 oz (55–85 gm) in weight, and about the size of an egg. If you save seed potatoes from your own crops there is a chance of virus diseases rapidly building up in the stock and progressively reducing future yields. These virus diseases are spread by greenfly, but disease-free stocks for British gardeners are grown in Scotland and Northern Ireland where the climatic conditions prevent the presence of aphis (greenfly). It is certainly advisable to buy 'Certified' disease-free seed potatoes.

Sometimes farmers save their own seed, planting what are known as

Potatoes can be stored in sacks for winter use.

'once-grown seed' – in other words planting tubers grown once outside the aphis-free areas. Where seed potatoes are very expensive you may want to risk saving your own seed-tubers for one year, but generally speaking it is not worth the risk of viruses which will considerably reduce the yield. There are many varieties of certified disease-free seed potatoes which are sold grouped according to their speed of maturity as 'Earlies', 'Second Earlies' and 'Maincrop', and it is certainly advisable to select one of these.

If your seed potatoes are larger than the ideal you can cut them to make two or more planting pieces as long as every piece has its own shoot (see figure 105).

A good way to increase the yield and get slightly earlier crops is to place the seed potatoes in trays in a warm (50°F (10°C)) light position for six to eight weeks before planting. During this time they will produce short dark green shoots. This pre-planting sprouting is called chitting. Whether chitted or not, plant the tubers in rows with a trowel 4–5 in (10–12 cm) deep, 12–15 in (30–38 cm) apart, with 24 in (60 cm) between the rows. Begin planting outdoors in late March/early April – or four to five weeks before the last frost is likely to occur. Some gardeners prefer to pull out a 4–5 in (10–12 cm) deep U-shaped drill with a hoe, along which they space out the tubers and then cover them with the soil. Choose whichever system suits you best.

Figure 106: Plant tubers in furrows and cover them with soil.

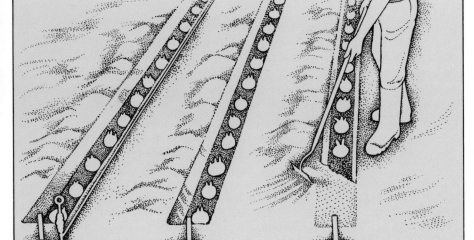

Figure 107: Earth up around the growing stems.

avoid cutting into the potatoes. Once the foliage starts to turn yellow and die down it is best to lift all the potatoes. Leave them on the surface of the soil for an hour or so, then put them in bags and store in a frost-free but cool place for use through the winter.

Possible Problems
In very damp conditions in the autumn the disease, potato blight, can be troublesome. This causes dark spots on the leaves and premature yellowing of the leaves. The spores drop from the leaves and infect the tubers which then develop soft brown rot in store. You can prevent this by growing early varieties and lifting them early.

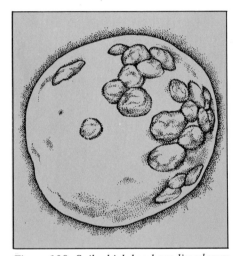
Figure 108: Soil which has been limed may produce tubers with scabs.

How to Grow
When the young shoots appear above the ground, draw up soil from between the rows around the stems. This is called 'earthing up'. If young shoots have come through and frosts are still likely, pull the soil right over them to give protection. Alternatively you can protect against frost by covering the rows with cloches or just covering with sacking on nights when frost is forecast.

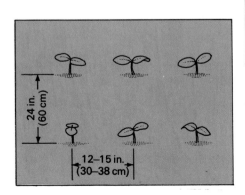

Repeat the earthing-up process several times as the crop grows. This increases the roots made by the potato stems and so gives a greater yield as well as helping to control weeds. It also keeps the developing tubers covered with soil and shaded from light which would turn them green and make them inedible.

USEFUL TIPS

1. For very early crops plant a few seed potato tubers in pots filled with potting compost and grow them in the greenhouse, sun lounge or glass-sided porch. Put one to three tubers in an 8 in (20 cm) pot — more tubers will give more small early potatoes.
2. An interesting way to grow potatoes on the 10 ft × 12 ft (3 m × 4 m) vegetable plot is to set the sprouting tubers on the surface of the cropping site and cover them with a 2 ft (60 cm) wide strip of black polythene. Bury the edges of the polythene to hold it in place and make a small slit in it above each tuber to let the potato shoots through. No earthing up is needed and the black polythene keeps the tubers from going green. The new potatoes are mostly produced on the surface and to gather them lift one edge of the polythene and pick the biggest potatoes.

Harvesting
Towards mid- to the end of July, move some soil away from the roots by hand to check the size of the new potatoes. When they are large enough to eat, start lifting them and keep the fork or spade well back from the plants to

Sprouted tubers being covered with black polythene sheet.

Alternatively, use a protective copper-based spray in early July.

Reduce the possibility of potatoes getting 'scabs' (brown corky patches on the skin) by adding plenty of organic matter but *no* lime, to the soil before planting. For example, it helps to scatter lawn mowings into the row at planting time.

A heavy crop of potatoes.

Pumpkins and Gourds

Pumpkins (*Cucurbita maxima*) can be grown to eat as a vegetable or made into pumpkin pie – a favourite American dish. They are also traditionally carved into ghostly faces to provide Hallowe'en decorations. More decorative but not grown to eat, are ornamental gourds which are now available in a great variety of shapes and colours. Both plants require the same cultural treatment, which is similar to that needed to grow marrows, and they are also not altogether suitable for the 10 ft × 12 ft (3 m × 4 m) vegetable plot as plants need a lot of space to grow.

Site and Soil
Both types of plants grow vigorously and require at least a couple of square yards (1·6 sq metres) on rich soil for each plant. A warm sunny site is needed to grow the largest pumpkins but smaller fruits can be grown in partially shaded sites. Dig plenty of organic matter into the soil to supply the moisture needed for rapid growth. A well rotted down compost heap provides an ideal site and rooting medium.

Pumpkins.

USEFUL TIP
Ornamental gourds look very effective trained up and over a trellis or fence. On terraces and balconies they can be grown in polythene bags filled with fertilised peat, or in compost-filled window boxes.

Sowing Instructions
Sow the seeds indoors in April/early May, two seeds per 3½ in (9 cm) pot. When seedlings are big enough to handle thin out to one per pot. Plant out when there is no more possibility of frost. You can also sow directly into the cropping site in late April/mid

Ornamental Gourds.

May. Cover the seeds with jam jars or cloches until the seedlings are established and the danger of frost has passed. Sow two or three seeds together at each point and thin down to one when the seedlings are big enough to handle. Sprinkle a little slug bait down after sowing out of doors as a precaution to prevent possible damage to the stems.

How to Grow
Keep the plants well watered in dry weather and give liquid feed every ten to fourteen days once the fruits begin to swell, to obtain the largest fruit. Pinch out the growing tip of the main stem to encourage more fruit bearing side shoots to form. A pumpkin plant will carry four or five fruits, but reduce this number to one or two per plant if you want really big pumpkins. You can encourage roots to be made from the stem and increase fruit size even more by heaping fertile soil over the fruit-bearing side shoots.

Where flowers open but fail to set fruit, you should hand-pollinate them. Pick a male flower (it will have no immature fruit behind the flower), remove the petals and push the yellow pollen-bearing anthers into a female flower, (which does have an embryo fruit behind the flower).

Harvesting
This will be in the late summer or early autumn. Leave the pumpkins on the stem to mature and ripen. If the fruit is not quite ripe and there is a possibility of frost, cover it with sacking overnight. If you want your pumpkins for Hallowe'en decorations, cut them a couple of weeks beforehand and just leave them on the soil. This really toughens the skin.

Gather gourds as they ripen and go hard which will be in late summer. Cut with secateurs and leave them in a dry, sunny position to dry.

Possible Problems
Watch out for mice and rats which will eat the seeds at sowing time and also the fruits left outside to ripen.

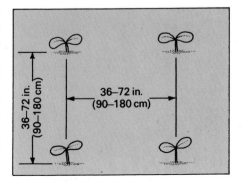

Radishes

Only mustard and cress is easier to grow than summer radish (*Raphanus sativus*). All you have to do is scatter seed on the ground, rake it in and, in warm weather, you will have succulent radishes ready for pulling within four weeks. The slight peppery flavour gives a spicey lift to salads and the bright scarlet skins of many varieties add colour to the green of other salad vegetables.

There are two kinds of radish: the best known, which could be described as ordinary radish, can be cropped from late April to November. The other type – the winter radish – may be black or red skinned and is much larger than the ordinary radish. It looks rather like a small turnip, and as it is completely hardy it can be stored and used through the winter.

Varieties

For summer cropping there are three main types – the globe-shaped, which may be scarlet or scarlet-tipped white; the oval or cylinder shaped, which is red with a white tip, and includes one of the most popular varieties, called 'French Breakfast'; and the long-rooted variety, which includes the aptly named 'White Icicle'. This produces pure white roots like slender pointed fingers.

Winter supplies are also provided by three varieties – probably the best known of which is 'Chinese Rose'. The 5–6 in (12·5–15 cm) long roots have white-tipped rose skin and grow up to 2 in (5 cm) in diameter. The other two varieties, 'Black Spanish Round' and 'Black Spanish Long', are about the same size as 'Chinese Rose' but they both have black skins. The

Long Black Radish.

Globe Radish.

flesh of all three types is white and their flavours are comparable.

Site and Soil

Radishes will grow anywhere in all reasonably well cultivated soils, from mid-spring to early autumn. The crispest and best flavoured radishes are those that are grown quickly, and speedy growth is most easily achieved on fertile soil in an open sunny position. If they are grown in light, dry soils and very overshadowed sites, the roots may be slow to swell and they tend to be very hot and rather woody.

Special Siting

Radishes grow so quickly there is no need to make special plans for them. Place short rows between slower maturing crops in the 10 ft × 12 ft (3 m × 4 m) vegetable plot; early in spring, for example, you can sow radish on either side of a row of emerging peas. Later in the year grow them between emerging runner beans and developing celery or brussels sprouts. This is known as 'catch-cropping', or the crop is described as an 'intercrop'.

You can grow small quantities in window boxes, and in greenhouse border soil among lettuce and tomatoes. If you are growing tomatoes and other crops in fertilised peat-filled polythene growing bags, you can also get in a quick crop of radish.

Sowing Instructions

In temperate areas start sowing the ordinary radish as soon as soil conditions allow. You should be able to sow under polythene cloches in February, but don't sow outside without protection until March. Draw shallow drills 6 in (15 cm) apart and sow the seed thinly down the row. Sow in succession every ten to fourteen days from early spring to September to provide crops from late April to November.

Sow winter radish in July, *not* before, in rows 12 in (30 cm) apart. Thin out the seedlings as they develop, to stand 6–8 in (15–20 cm) apart in the row.

How to Grow

Radishes really are 'instant gardening', and once you have sown the seed there is very little more you have to do. Some shade may be needed from very hot sun in midsummer and in order to maintain a supply of succulent radish make sure they have plenty of moisture. You can provide shade by replacing the strip of polythene on polythene tunnel cloches with net curtain.

Harvesting

Start pulling up the roots as soon as the ordinary radish are large enough – about ½ in (1·5 cm) in diameter. Take out the largest ones first (you can see which they are by pushing the leaves gently to one side and selecting the thickest roots). The smaller roots that you leave behind will grow quickly to give a succession of radishes.

Start pulling winter radish in November and store the roots in peat or sand. You can also leave them in the soil and pull as you require them, but remember that in very hard, frosty weather pulling will be difficult. You should also protect them with straw.

USEFUL TIP

The radish is a very useful indicator crop to help you to plot slow-to-germinate items. For example, if you sow a mixture of radish and parsley seed in the same row, the radishes grow quickly and soon show just where the seed was situated. This allows you to hoe between rows to control weeds without disturbing the parsley seeds. The radishes will have grown and been pulled to eat by the time the parsley is established and requires all the space. Sowings of onion, parsnip and carrot are good examples of where indicator crops are a help.

French Breakfast Radish.
Long White Radish.

Possible Problems

Radishes are grouped in the same family as cabbages and all the brassicas, so they are susceptible to the same pests and diseases – for example clubroot. Try and plant on disease-free soil, but as the plants grow so quickly any subsequent signs of trouble are best cured by destroying the crop and making another quick sowing in fresh soil.

One problem which you may need to control is attack by flea beetles – small shiny black insects which eat neat round holes in the seedling leaves. This pest is a problem with all the cabbage and turnip family when soil conditions are hot and dry. You can control it by dusting with BHC early in the morning, while the leaves still carry some dew. The dust sticks to it and is more effective.

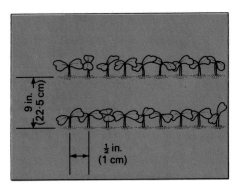

Rhubarb

There is heated debate in some horticultural circles on the classification of rhubarb (*Rheum rhaponticum*), which is grown very much like a vegetable and yet the bright pink stems are used as a tart acid-flavoured alternative to fruit in many desserts. Because it features in the corner of many suburban vegetable plots, we include cultural details here. Remember, it is only the stems of the plant which are eaten – the green leaves contain poisonous oxalic acid.

Site and Soil

Rhubarb thrives in any site – however bad and all reasonably cultivated garden soil will give good results. The better the soil and the cultural treatment, however, the greater will be the yield of stems and those soils which retain moisture to support the rapid leafy growth in hot weather are the ideal. Once again you can help water retention by adding plenty of well-rotted compost to the soil. Waterlogged soils are best avoided.

Sowing and Propagation

You can raise rhubarb from seed sown outdoors in March in drills 1–2 in (2·5–5 cm) deep and 12 in (30 cm) apart, but plants raised in this way are almost certain to be inferior to named varieties propagated by division. They also take two or three seasons before they are large enough to provide leaf stems which can be pulled.

To propagate three to five year old plants of named varieties, lift them during the dormant period, November to March, and chop them with a spade to produce five or six planting pieces.

Figure 110: Rhubarb set. (Above) Rhubarb being prepared for the table.

These are called 'sets'. Each set must have one rounded pink bud and a fair share of root system; as a guide a planting piece should be about the size of a man's hand. It may be as well to cut through the very largest buds as these invariably produce a flower stalk the first year. Sets with one or more smaller buds will develop into strong plants the first year.

How to Grow

Dig the soil well and clear it of perennial weeds before planting the sets 2½ ft (75 cm) apart (October and March are good times to plant). Occasional hoeing to control weeds is the only other cultural treatment you need to do, but you can improve growth and yield by putting compost, manure and general fertiliser around the plants. January is the time to apply manure and compost and April the time to give fertiliser. Plants can be left down to crop for up to twenty years but in practice replacing in fresh soil every five or so years maintains good yields and keeps plants to manageable size.

You can get early crops by encouraging early growth (known as forced growth). To do this either cover the plants in the soil with boxes filled with straw or lift the whole crown, surround it with damp peat or soil and grow it in a warm dark atmosphere. Succulent bright pink blanched stems are produced by forced plants. All rhubarb crowns need a period of cold, frosty weather before forcing, so leave

lifted crowns exposed to the frost before boxing and bringing them indoors to force. It is best to discard crowns after forcing.

Harvesting

Leave the plants for one season after planting. In the second year you can start to pull the stems, but don't denude the plant of leaves if you plan to crop for a number of years. Just pull up the leaf stems which are large enough to use and they will come cleanly away from the plant. Then cut off the leaves and the rhubarb stems are ready for use. Always leave a few leaves on the plant after pulling.

Possible Problems

None to worry about.

USEFUL TIP

Watch out for new 'disease cleaned up' varieties which are likely to give heavier yields.

Figure 109: 3- or 4-year-old rhubarb crowns may be chopped to make sets.

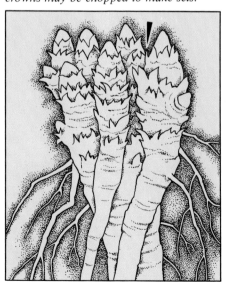

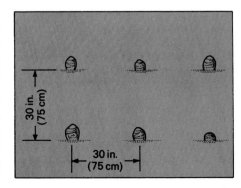

30 in. (75 cm)
30 in. (75 cm)

Salsify, Scorzonera and Seakale

These two less common root vegetables – Salsify, (*Tragopogon porrifolius*) which has rush-like leaves, and Scorzonera, (*Scorzonera hispanica*) which has broader strap-shaped leaves — are quite easy to grow. They require similar treatment both in the garden and the kitchen, but it is easy to distinguish between the two. Scorzonera roots have a black skin which can be removed by scalding and scraping. Salsify is a similar shape, but the roots are brown, not black. This vegetable is commonly called the 'Vegetable Oyster' because of its flavour. The roots of both vegetables have a very subtle, delicate flavour and they are prepared for eating by either boiling in salted water or slicing and frying.

Scorzonera.

Salsify.

Site and Soil

Choose an open site and ideally a deep, well-cultivated soil to which you have added well-rotted manure for previous crops. The kind of soils which produce good carrots and parsnips are likely to produce good salsify and scorzonera roots.

Sowing Instructions

Sow from March to early May in rows 12–15 in (30–38 cm) apart. A good long growing season is needed for plump roots.

How to Grow

Thin the seedlings to stand 6–9 in (15–23 cm) apart in the row when they are big enough to handle. Hoe occasionally to control weeds and water the plants well in dry weather.

Harvesting

Roots will be ready for lifting from mid-October, but be careful when lift-ing salsify as damaged roots will bleed and lose their flavour. Lift the roots as you require them or lift them carefully in November and store in peat or sand. See that all lifted roots are adequately protected during storage so they remain plump and do not shrivel (which also reduces the flavour).

A few roots of salsify can be left in the soil to produce tender young shoots in spring. These shoots can be left green or blanched by covering them with a flower pot. Cut when they are 6 in (15 cm) or so high and cook them in the same way as you would asparagus. One row along the 10 ft (3 m) edge of the plot will provide enough roots for at least twenty, average-sized servings.

Possible Problems

None to worry about.

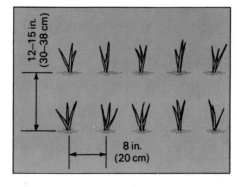

USEFUL TIP

To get the best from salsify, lift and scrape the roots immediately before you want them for cooking. After scraping and before cooking, put the roots into cold water to which you have added a little lemon juice.

SEAKALE

Seakale (*Crambe maritima*) is another unusual vegetable which is forced in winter to produce blanched leaf stems.

Site and Soil

All sites for seakale need to be well-cultivated. Improve poor soils by adding well-rotted organic matter.

Sowing and Propagating

You can sow seed in March/April but plants grown from seed will not be ready to force for two years. The faster

Seakale.

method is to propagate from root cuttings (called thongs). These should be 6–8 in (15–23 cm) long and are cut from roots which have been lifted to force. Keep in sand, (tops uppermost) until spring planting time.

How to Grow

Thin seedlings and space thongs 18 in (45 cm) apart, covering the thongs with 1 in (2·5 cm) of soil.

Harvesting

Either cover the roots with straw or an upturned flower pot in situ to force, or put roots in deep boxes of damp peat.

Possible Problems

None to worry about.

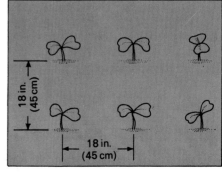

Sorrel and Spinach

SORREL

Common sorrel, which has arrow-shaped leaves and green, turning to red, flower spikes, may be found growing wild, but it is the larger-leaved 'French Sorrel' (*Rumex scutatus*) which may be cultivated in gardens. The leaves are paler coloured and not so tart and make good flavouring for soups, fish sauces, omelettes and salads.

Site and Soil

Sorrel will grow in any well drained site in sun and partial shade. All lime-free soils are acceptable. The natural presence of sorrel indicates an acid soil. Add plenty of peat or flowers of sulphur to the soil to increase its acidity content.

Sowing and Propagating

Either sow seed outdoors in April or divide and replant establish plants in March/April and September. Space the rows 15–18 in (45 cm) apart and the plants 9 in (23 cm) apart in the row. If you are growing from seed, thin the seedlings to this distance apart.

How to Grow

Pick out the flower spikes as they develop and hoe between plants to control weeds.

Harvesting

Gather the leaves young (after about six to eight weeks) for the tenderest and mildest flavour. Such leaves can be dried or deep frozen to provide year round supplies.

Spinach.

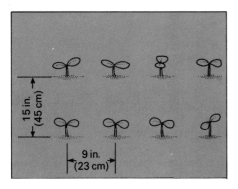

SPINACH
SPINACH BEET
AND NEW ZEALAND SPINACH

'Spinach Beet' and 'New Zealand Spinach' (*Tetragonia expansa*) are not botanically true *Spinacia*, but they are grown to provide a leaf vegetable. It is therefore usual to consider them together with Spinach, (*Spinacia oleracea*).

SUMMER AND WINTER SPINACH

The annual spinach is one of the fastest maturing leaf vegetables and is ideal to grow as an intercrop between slower maturing vegetables such as celery and leeks. The tender young leaves of spinach should be chopped and *steamed* to present an appetising vegetable. If boiled in quantities of water, a wet unpalatable 'slush' is the disappointing result.

Varieties

There are two main groups – the round or smooth-seeded 'Summer Spinach' which includes such varieties as 'Long-Standing Round', and the rough or prickly-seeded 'Winter Spinach', such as the variety 'Long-Standing Prickly'. Recently introduced varieties like 'Sigmaleaf' have round seed and can be used for both summer and winter cropping.

Site and Soil

Full sun or partial shade are both acceptable and the best soil is a really good moisturing-retaining type. Light, dry soils and hot weather make plants run prematurely to seed.

Sowing Instructions

To get continuous cropping, sow summer spinach successively every fourteen days from February to July and winter spinach in August and September. Sow the seed thinly in drills 1 in (2·5 cm) deep and 12–15 in (30–38 cm) apart. Thin the seedlings first to stand 3 in (7·5 cm) apart and then thin again after about a month to 6–12 in (15–30 cm) apart. Winter spinach is not as vigorous growing so the closer spacing is quite adequate. Plants from the second thinning will be of edible size. Keep the seedlings well watered in dry weather to obtain the fastest growth.

Sorrel.

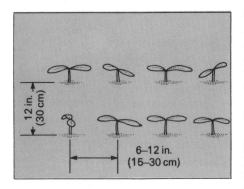

How to Grow
Hoe to control weeds and water well in dry weather. Protect winter spinach from frost by covering with cloches from November.

Harvesting
As soon as the leaves are large enough (summer spinach from May onwards, winter spinach from mid-November) start to gather them, picking the largest ones first. Don't strip the plant, in fact harvest no more than half the leaves at a time, leaving smaller leaves to develop, (although don't leave them too long, or the leaves will be old and tough). Gather leaves by pinching through the leaf stalks; don't pull them off as this may damage the roots. Summer spinach will supply the period May to October, and as it grows more vigorously will stand heavier picking than winter spinach.

Possible Problems
None to worry about. If the leaves of summer spinach turn yellow for any reason, just pull up infected plants and make another sowing.

USEFUL TIP
Summer spinach is an excellent snatch crop for fertilised peat-filled growing bags. It will be ready to pick in seven weeks from sowing.

NEW ZEALAND SPINACH
The spreading plants of New Zealand Spinach are often called 'cut-and-come-again' because they provide a continuous supply of leafy shoots. The photographs on this page clearly show the difference in leaf shape between this and spinach – the New Zealand Spinach has smaller and not such shiny leaves. Apart from its trailing habit, this plant is also different from ordinary spinach because it is *not* frost-hardy, but it will withstand dry soil conditions without forming premature flower spikes.

Site and Soil
Most garden sites and soils will give acceptable results but sunny positions and light well drained soils will give the best growth and heaviest picking of foliage.

Sowing Instructions
For the earliest crops, sow indoors in pots in late March/early April and plant out, after the possibility of frost, in May or June. Sow the main-crop outside in early May (only one sowing is necessary). Space the rows 2–2½ ft (60–75 cm) apart and the plants 18–24 in (45–60 cm) down the row.

How to Grow
Maintain rapid growth by constant watering in dry weather. Pinch out the growing tips, especially those that form early in the season, to encourage the development of side shoots. These will produce more leaves to harvest.

Harvesting
Leaves will be ready to gather in six to seven weeks from a May sowing. Try to pick the leaves singly to allow the development of further leaves along each stem.

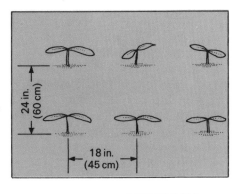

SPINACH BEET or PERPETUAL SPINACH
The easiest of all the spinach type plants to grow, this is a hardy biennial root crop and will stand through the winter. If you have had difficulties growing other spinach crops, just try this one.

Site and Soil
Any site is suitable but try and avoid those which are heavily overshadowed. All cultivated garden soils are suitable but preferably should not be too wet in the winter.

Sowing Instructions
Sow outdoors in April for the summer crops and in July/August for winter and spring cropping. Sow the seed in

New Zealand Spinach.

drills about 1 in (2·5 cm) deep, in rows 15 in (38 cm) apart.

How to Grow
Thin the seedlings to stand 6–9 in (15–23 cm) apart as soon as they are large enough to handle. You can speed leaf production in hot weather by watering in a top dressing of general fertiliser, or alternatively giving a good liquid feed.

Harvesting
Gather the larger leaves by pulling the leaf stalk gently away from the root. Pick regularly but not too hard, leaving some young central leaves to help the plant to continue growing. Throw old outer leaves on to the compost heap. In a mild autumn, the July/August sowings may provide some late autumn/early winter leaves, but do not pick these too hard because plant strength needs to be built up for good spring crops.

Possible Problems
None to worry about, but should leaf miner attack plants by tunnelling through the leaves, just pinch the maggots to destroy them.

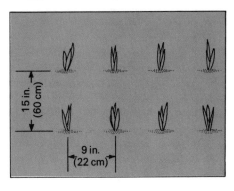

Sweet Corn

Commonly called 'Corn on the Cob', sweet corn (*Zea mays*) is a very popular vegetable well worth growing in warm places. It is a perfect vegetable for deep freezing, but, particularly if you want it for this purpose, don't leave the cobs on the plant to get old and starchy. To freeze, pop the cobs into boiling water for seven to ten minutes, cool in cold running water and then cut the grain from the stem. Put into plastic bags or deep freeze containers and place in freezer.

Site and Soil
Select a warm sheltered site in cooler districts – plenty of sun and well cultivated garden soil are the growing requirements. Add plenty of well-rotted organic matter to poor soils to improve moisture retention.

Special Siting
If you want a temporary screen in the garden plant strong-growing varieties like 'John Innes Hybrid'. Plants will grow to 4–5 ft (120–150 cm) high.

Sowing Instructions
Sow indoors in pots (peat pots are the best) in late April/early May. Plant in the cropping site under cloches in late May or unprotected when the risk of frost has passed. Alternatively sow directly into the cropping site from mid-May, placing two or three seeds every 12–15 in (30–38 cm) down the row – the rows 15–30 in (38–76 cm) apart. If you are growing the tall, strong-growing varieties you will need the wider spacing.

How to Grow
Thin seedlings to one, once established. If you are growing them under cloches, remove these when the leaves touch the top and the possibility of frost has passed. Pollen from the male tassels which form at the top of the plant floats down in the wind to pollinate the female cobs which are formed in a sheath of leaves lower down the

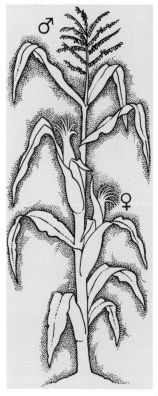

Figure 111: Male and female flowers. (Above) Sweet Corn Cobs.

plant. Complete wind pollination is more likely if you grow plants in a block of several rows, rather than in a single row. Hoe to control weeds and as you do so, draw up some soil round the base of the stem. This encourages firm rooting. Remove basal side shoots so that all the strength is directed into the main stem.

USEFUL TIP

Seek out the dwarf, early, F_1 hybrids for small compact plants to grow in the 10 ft × 12 ft (3 × 4 m) vegetable plot.

Harvesting
A double row of the dwarf F_1 hybrid varieties such as 'Earliking' along the 10 ft (3 m) edge of the plot will yield more than twenty cobs which ripen through August and September. When the female thread-like stigmas protruding from the green sheath turn dark brown and black, ease the leafy bracts back gently to see if the grains of corn are ready. When ripe, a white milky sap will flow from the grain if you puncture it with your thumb nail. If the sap is clear and the grains small, the cob is not ready; if there is no moist sap, the grains have become too old and will be starchy. To gather, snap the ripe cobs from the stem.

Peel away the husk and female

threads before cooking the cobs in salted water. Each plant should produce two or three cobs and you should restrict all but the strongest-growing plants to growing only this number.

Possible Problems
Frit fly maggots often burrow into the growing point of the plant early in the year causing twisted leaves and stunted growth. You can eliminate this problem by raising plants indoors.

Figure 112: Grow sweet corn in blocks for good wind pollination.

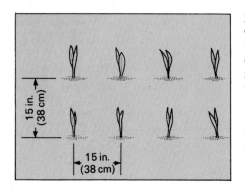

Tomatoes

The introduction in recent years of new varieties and new growing techniques for tomatoes (*Lycopersicon esculentum*) has meant that there is no reason why everyone should not have home – or even office – grown tomatoes from June to December each year. The only requirement is a window sill or small terraced or paved area outside. If you have a garden and/or greenhouse as well, you will be able to grow masses of fresh tomatoes.

Varieties
If you are not conversant with the multitude of varieties now available, try to sort the seedman's list into groups. The best known are what I like to call the *ordinary* round tomatoes which grow on single stemmed plants. Varieties include well known and proven names like 'Ailsa Craig' and 'Moneymaker', which have served the gardener well for years, both outdoors and under cover.

More recently however, the introduction of F₁ hybrids has given advances in yield, quality and uniformity of growth. Good examples of F₁ hybrids in the 'ordinary' group are 'Ware Cross' (one of the first bred by the John Innes Institute), 'Eurocross A' and 'Eurocross BB' (extensively used by growers in the early 1970's). Still within this 'ordinary' group, but different in colour, are the yellow-fruited cultivars. These tend to be sweeter and of a more bland flavour, and include such varieties as 'Golden Sunrise' and 'Golden Queen'.

In the second group are the outdoor varieties, including all the hardier and early maturing types. Heading the list is the variety 'Outdoor Girl', the leaves of which look more like potatoes than tomatoes.

Grouped as equally suitable for indoor and outdoor culture, are the bushy multi-stemmed kinds. These include 'Pixie' F₁ (2–2½ ft (60–75 cm)); 'Gardener's Delight' sometimes known as 'Sugar Plum' (2 ft (60 cm)); 'The Amateur' (18 in–2 ft (45–60 cm)) and 'Tiny Tim' (15 in (38 cm)) high, which has very small round fruits and is ideal to grow in a 5 in (13 cm) pot on the window sill or on a balcony or patio.

Finally there are the very 'offbeat' kinds of tomato which range from the variety 'Small Fry' F₁, with its marble sized fruits and the giant-fruited 'Big Boy' F₁, to the red and yellow striped fruits of 'Tigerella' and various pear-shaped fruited varieties.

Figure 113: Remove side shoots as they form to direct energy into plant.

Site and Soil
Sunshine is the one real requirement for good tomato growing. The brighter the light, particularly early in the year when raising young plants, the better the growth and the better the flavour. Tomatoes are tender plants that will not stand any frost, and if grown without protection they need a warm spot in sheltered gardens, such as a south-facing wall or fence. Cloche protection, glass-sided porches, home extensions and cold greenhouses will all lengthen the growing and cropping season. Heated greenhouses extend the season even further, and if minimum night temperatures of 60°–65°F (15°–18°C) can be maintained, crops can be gathered more or less the whole year round.

Well-cultivated garden soils improved by the addition of well-rotted manure and other organic materials are best for tomatoes, although all garden soils are likely to give acceptable results. Use any of the proprietary potting composts to fill pots and similar growing containers. The richer the compost used, (up to John Innes No 3 strength), the longer will be the period before you have to give liquid feeding.

Special Siting
Use a little imagination and there is no end to the places where tomatoes can be grown – dwarf varieties in window boxes and hanging baskets for example. (If you are using the smaller hanging baskets, regular liquid feeding will be necessary).

Very good crops will grow in greenhouse border soil, but some crop rotation must be practised. After two or three years of growing in the same soil, you must either change the soil or introduce another growing method or crop (see rotation charts), if you are to

'Ordinary' Tomatoes – note the fresh green calyces.

Miniature Tomatoes.

maintain the same weight of cropping.

Ring culture is one alternative growing method. Stand 9–12 in (23–30 cm) diameter bottomless pots or rings on an isolated bed of aggregate (gravel, coarse ash, crushed stone) and fill them with John Innes No 3 potting compost (see figure 114). Plants grown in these obtain food from the ring, and water from the aggregate. After planting, water well and then leave for several days for the plants to root through the compost and out into the aggregate. Water the compost sparingly for ten to twelve days then water the aggregate regularly. Start liquid feeding once the fruit starts to swell.

Using polythene fertilised peat-filled bags is an easier method, and they give equally heavy cropping. Put the bags down on the cropping site, which could be a terrace, a greenhouse or a balcony for example. Cut holes in the upper surface of the bag, water through these and then put in the plants. Once you have got the amount of watering right, 'grow-bag' tomato growing is very easy, and you can check water requirements by tearing off a piece of newspaper and pressing this with your thumb against the surface of the peat. If the moisture comes through the paper no watering is necessary; if the paper remains dry, you need to water.

Sowing Instructions

It is quite easy to raise a few plants from seed on the window sill. The secret is not to sow too soon because checks to growth from cold are likely if you are forced to plant out and pot on into conditions when the night temperature is below 50°F (10°C). Allow approximately six to eight weeks to raise plants, which for most crops means a March/April sowing. Use any seed compost and sow seeds approximately ½–1 in (1–2·5 cm) apart.

When the first two seed leaves have unfolded, lift the seedlings and space them singly in 3½ in (9 cm) pots filled with any good potting compost, (such as John Innes No 1). You can either put the plants out into soil when they are 6–9 in (15–23 cm) high or pot on into larger pots and containers.

How to Grow

Start to liquid feed every ten to fourteen days when the plants are carrying four trusses.

You will probably come across the terms 'single stemmed cordon' and 'stopping' if you read cultural notes for tomatoes. Cordon growing and single stemmed refer to the same thing – that is supporting a plant by tying it to a cane, stake or twining round a string and removing every side shoot which forms at the joint between leaf and stem. If these side shoots are not removed – a practice known as side shooting or trimming – they tend to grow away vigorously at the expense of the adjacent flower truss.

Very young side shoots can easily be rubbed out with your fingers, but if by mistake you leave them to get larger – say beyond pencil thickness – then it is better to cut them out with a knife.

Early in the life of tomato plants, especially those in rich soil and compost, the growing tip of the plant will

Pear-shaped Tomatoes.

be very dark green, and the leaf stalks and leaves will be thick and curled right round. This presents no cause for alarm and in fact is a good sign of very vigorous growth. You need do nothing to the growing tip until you feel the plant has enough fruit. Outdoor plants in Britain for example have a growing season only long enough to allow four or at the most five trusses to develop, at which point you must remove the growing tip. This is known as stopping, and it ensures that all the plant's energies are directed into the fruit. If growing under cold glass, each plant can support at least six to eight trusses.

Give the plants a tap on the stem at midday, and syringe with water in sunny conditions to improve pollination and fruit set. Alternatively, spray

Figure 114: Growing tomatoes in the ring culture system.

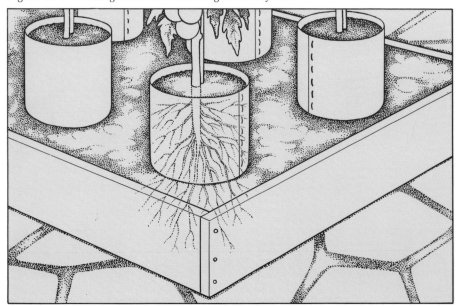

Golden Tomato.

Giant Fruited Tomato.

the flowers with special fruit setting chemical to be sure fruit development will follow. Flowers failing to set is usually the lack of light affecting very early crops. You should have no problem with later planted crops from an April sowing, and there is no need to tap or spray.

Harvesting

Once the lower leaves start to turn yellow with age it is best to trim them off with a sharp knife so that sun and air can get to the ripening fruit. The flavour will be best if you pick the fruit when it is firm but ripe, and eat it fresh from the plant! Lift the fruit, placing your thumb or finger nail at the little angled joint on the stem just above the green spidery calyx, and it will snap off easily without damaging the truss or the stem of the plant.

At the end of the growing season and before the possibility of frost, cut down the plants, leaving any ungathered fruit on the stems, and hang in a frost-free place to ripen. Alternatively, untie outdoor plants, place them on straw and cover with cloches to extend the ripening period.

Another method for late autumn/early winter 'off-the-plant-ripening' is to cut off the trusses and place them in trays in a cool, (45°–50°F (10°C)) dark position. Green fruit gathered in this

way will provide you with a succession of ripening fruit through to Christmas. You can speed up ripening by raising the temperature, but it also increases the risk of the fruit shrivelling.

Possible Problems

If the leaves turn yellow on plants soon after you have planted them out, or the stems turn blue and growth ceases, either the night temperatures are too low or the soil is too cold and too wet. Raising the temperature and planting later are the remedies.

Black patches on the base of fruit, (a condition called 'Blossom End Rot') is caused by careless watering. Make sure your plants never suffer from lack of water, especially when they are carrying a heavy crop of fruit.

Yellow spots on the leaf surface and soft purple-grey mould on the underside is caused by leaf mould. Control this disease either by using resistant varieties or spraying with copper, maneb or zineb fungicide.

You can control greenfly and whitefly, which leave black sticky mould on the leaves, with Resmethrin-based and similar insecticides.

If the plants with several trusses of fruit suddenly wilt in hot weather on soil which has produced several crops of tomatoes, they probably have the disease Verticilium Wilt. If the plant has collapsed completely, cut open the stem at ground level and you will find a brown stain line. A deep mulch of peat or compost around the stem will encourage new roots to form and may salvage some of the crop. Avoid using the same soil again.

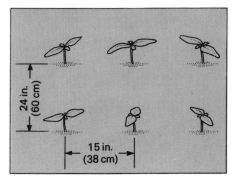

Turnips

The turnip (*Brassica rapa*) is one of those crops which need to be pulled young to give the most appetising cooked vegetable. Plants which have grown quickly and are gathered in early summer are delicious and may be cooked and served whole or diced to complement other succulent root vegetables like carrots.

Varieties

There is quite a range of varieties to choose from, the main differences between them being in colour and shape. The most popular types are those known as 'flat round' roots; the top and bottom of the root is flat but the remaining root area is globe-shaped. The best example of this type is the variety called 'White Milan'. Flat-topped varieties in which only the top half is coloured, such as 'Green-top White' and 'Purple Milan' are also available. In addition to these there are the true globe-shaped varieties like the white 'Snowball' and 'Golden Ball'. Less common but useful for growing early under cloches are the long cylinder shaped varieties like the white-rooted 'Jersey Navet'.

Site and Soil

Any garden site is suitable, but avoid those that are heavily shaded. All well cultivated garden soils are suitable, but the best shaped roots grow in soil that has been manured and enriched for previous crops. Plenty of organic matter in the soil gives the rapid root growth necessary for the production of succulent roots. They are fast growing crops and will be ready for pulling in seven to eight weeks, so use turnips as catch crops, i.e. sow a row on any spare

Flat Round Turnip.

Purple Topped Turnip.

soil before or after slower maturing vegetables.

Sowing Instructions

Sow successionally from February under cloches and outside from late March/early April, every three weeks to July. These sowings will mature in about eight to twelve weeks – the warmer the weather the faster the maturity – and the roots should be lifted to eat young and fresh. Late July/early August sowings will provide maincrop roots to lift in November and store for winter use. Sow the seed in rows 12 in (30 cm) apart and cover very lightly with soil.

How to Grow

As the seedlings produce the first rough leaves, thin them out to stand 4 in (10 cm) apart along the row. Pull some early roots so that the remainder stand at 8 in (20 cm) apart. This two-stage harvesting is very useful to obtain young roots in early autumn, leaving the second for maincrop use. The only other attention needed is occasional hoeing to control weeds.

Harvesting

Start pulling the young turnips as soon as they are large enough to cook. This should certainly be before they reach tennis ball size, which is as large as quality will allow. You can check the size by pushing the foliage aside with your hands – part of the root will be above ground. If they are allowed to grow big and old, they will be coarse and woody and the mustardy flavour will be too strong. Lift the maincrop roots carefully in November, screw off the tops (using your hands rather than a knife) and store in clamps and boxes of peat and sand.

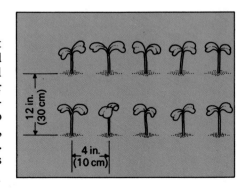

Possible Problems

As turnips belong to the brassica family, they can fall victim to the pests and diseases of cabbages and other green vegetables. Generally, however, they are very easy to grow and the only really likely problem is Flea Beetle attack. This pest loves hot dry conditions, so be particularly on the lookout if you are growing an early crop under a frame or cloches. Signs of attack are neat round holes in the young seedling leaves. BHC dust will give quick control. Apply it to the leaves in the early morning.

Split roots may occur, particularly if heavy rain or watering follows a dry period. The splitting will be worse if the crop was large enough to pull ahead of the dry spell.

Very swollen and distorted roots will be produced on soils infected by the disease club root. If the soil has been proved to contain this disease it is best to avoid growing turnips.

USEFUL TIPS

1. If turnip roots are left in store too long and produce blanched shoots, try cooking the shoots as a substitute for blanched seakale.
2. The fast-growing F₁ hybrid turnips such as 'Tokyo Cross' grow very well in fertilised, peat-filled growing bags. Very large roots can be produced, and because they have an ample water supply they retain the quality of small young roots grown in the open soil. After harvesting, another crop can be grown in the bags.

TURNIPS – grown for greens

Seedling turnips grown to provide a

Turnip Tops.

A variety of Golden Turnip.

fresh green vegetable full of iron were popular in the past and used to be a major crop in country cottage gardens. For some reason they have fallen out of favour in recent years, but with fresh winter and early spring vegetables usually in short supply, turnip greens deserve a return to popularity.

Site and Soil

Any cultivated soil is suitable. Choose a spot that is sheltered a little from the hardest of winter weather.

Sowing Instructions

Either scatter the seed over the surface soil and rake it in, or draw shallow drills 9–12 in (23–30 cm) apart, where weed growth might be a problem in late August/early September.

How to Grow

Leave the seedlings as you have sown them, do *not* thin them out. Apart from hoeing between the rows to control weeds, no cultural treatment is necessary.

Harvesting

Cut the leaves when they are 6–8 in (15–20 cm) high and cook in the same way as spinach or leafy spring greens. You can begin to gather them eight to ten weeks after sowing, although early spring is the main harvesting period.

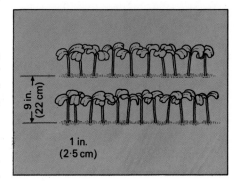

Pests and Diseases and their Control

The first and most important method of pest and disease control is to try to cultivate on strong, vigorously growing, healthy plants. Invariably it is the weaker growing specimens which fall first to the onslaught of pest and disease, and given this pocket of infection, the trouble will rapidly spread to adjacent, stronger plants.

This spread of infection emphasizes the importance of garden hygiene. Single diseased plants are, as a general rule, best removed and destroyed, either by burning, or better still by sealing in a polythene bag which is disposed of in the dustbin.

Weeds as well as vegetables offer comfortable accommodation for pests and disease, so it is essential to keep the plot as free as possible from weeds. For the same reason the ground should be cleared of all crops once harvesting is complete. The dying remains of plants – be it leaves, stems, roots and seed pods are perfect pest and disease building spots and should therefore be cleared on to the compost heap and rolled down as soon as they are removed from the site.

Even where good growing and this kind of hygiene is carried out, the occasional pest and disease problem is possible and when this happens I see no harm in resorting to chemical control. It is very important, however, *to follow absolutely the instructions given by the manufacturers*. Be sure to keep concentrated chemicals and sprays away from children and out of fish ponds.

Chemicals will control the problem either by direct contact or systemically, which means the chemical is first taken up by the plant and then works its pest and disease destruction from the sap. As systemic chemicals are carried right through the plant system, the chance of missed spots, as occurs with inadequate spraying and dusting with contact chemicals, is less likely.

If you are using chemical dusts, early morning applications when the plants are still damp with dew, are the most effective as they give a better chance of the dust sticking to leaves and stems of the plants. Apply liquid sprays of contact pesticides and fungicides evenly over the tops and undersides of leaves and stems to get as complete control as possible.

There are a number of chemicals which can be applied close to harvest time, but it may be necessary to leave the crop for a given period after spraying and before harvesting, with some of them. You must observe these periods and also be extra careful when spraying plants in flower. Bees, as well as pests, can be killed by some sprays, so if it is unavoidable to spray flowering plants do so in the evening when the bees are not active.

There are also several chemicals which can be mixed into the soil to give a long period of pest control. It is wise in all cases, however, to use only the amount that is absolutely necessary – prevention may be better than cure in most cases, but you should still avoid using pesticides and fungicides continuously. If you do use them repeatedly, the chance of building up resistance to the control chemical increases, thus reducing or losing altogether the effect of a good weapon in the garden chemical armoury. Ringing the changes and using alternative sprays is the best way to avoid the build-up of resistance, where a pest or disease problem persists.

Aphids.

PESTS AND THEIR CONTROL

Aphids: A pest commonly called 'greenfly' although there are black coloured flies, grey mealy cabbage aphis, rose aphis and several other types and shapes! Some of each kind have wings, others are wingless and they all breed at an alarming rate if not controlled. Some people recommend spraying them with soapy water, but all this does is wash them off the plant. Prompt destruction is better, and can be achieved with materials like derris, lindane and malathion. If you want to destroy aphis, but leave ladybirds and lacewings (which eat aphis) unharmed, use the very selective and fast acting pirimicarb (sold under the name Rapid).

Birds: Sparrows can be kept from pecking seedlings by stretching occasional strands of black cotton over the rows of emerging seedlings. Large nets placed over winter green crops are the best way to protect them from pigeons. A cat might frighten the birds

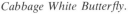

Cabbage White Butterfly.

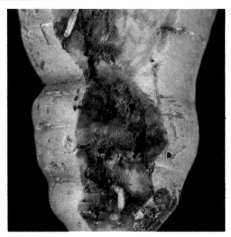

Carrot Fly.

but soil scratching and rolling cats can be a nuisance. (Deterrents like 'cat pepper' may be helpful to frighten cats off without harming them.)

Cabbage Root Fly: Small white maggots which feed on the roots of cabbage and other brassicas causing the plants to wilt. Crush all the maggots you can find to destroy them and either water plants with lindane or dip roots at transplanting time in calomel dust. You can also treat soil with bromophos and diazinon.

Turn to page 60 for a simple non-

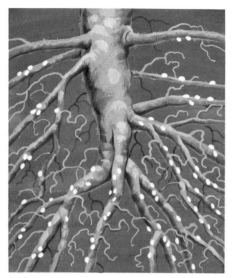

Eelworm.

chemical way of controlling cabbage root fly using a circular disc of rubber or similar material.

Cabbage White Butterfly: Green caterpillars which rapidly eat the leaves of all greens. Pick them off whenever you can and destroy them. Dust or spray plants with lindane, carbaryl, derris or similar material.

Carrot Fly: These tiny maggots which look like small wireworms, eat carrot and parsnip roots. Use seed dressings and treat the soil with bromophos and lindane to get control. (Early carrot crops are not affected.)

Celery Fly: This is a kind of leaf miner which causes brown spots on the leaves of celery and may also attack beetroot. Crush the larvae between your finger and thumb and spray the plant with malathion. Give liquid feed after spraying to help plants recover.

Flea Beetle.

Eelworm: These tiny larvae drastically reduce crops of potato, cucumbers and tomato. Chemical control is difficult in the garden, but strict rotation of crops coupled with the using of certified seed potatoes only should prevent attack.

Flea Beetle or Turnip Fly: Small shiny black beetles which jump if you brush your hand over seedlings. All brassica seedlings, including radish, are liable to attack in hot dry conditions, and indications are neat round holes appearing in the leaves. Seed dressing and lindane dust give control. Repeated evening watering will also help to prevent and control this pest.

Frit Fly: A larva which attacks sweet corn at the third seed leaf stage. You will avoid this pest if you raise plants indoors.

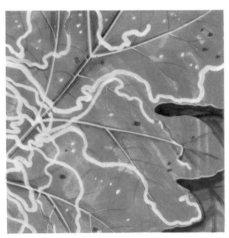

Leaf Miner.

Leaf Miner: Little white maggots which tunnel into the leaves of celery, beetroot and other crops – they can be killed by pinching with your thumb nail and by spraying the plant with lindane and malathion.

Leatherjackets: These greyish-brown grubs, which are plump and 1–1½ in (2·5–4 cm) long, are the larvae of daddy longlegs and eat the roots of seedlings. They are most likely to occur after digging up grass. If young plants begin to wilt, it may be because of attack by leatherjackets. Kill any larvae you find eating the roots.

Mice: Will eat newly sown seeds, especially peas and marrows. You can control them by putting mouse bait in old cans and placing these on their sides down the rows.

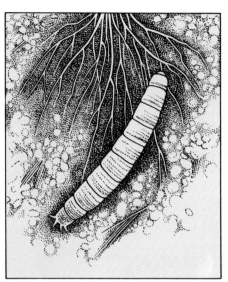

Leatherjacket.

Millipedes and Cutworms: Millipedes look like thinner, smaller leatherjackets, are slow moving and curl up when touched. Cutworms are lighter in colour and look more like caterpillars. Both eat through the roots of plants and may be controlled with soil pest killers like lindane, carbaryl (sold under the name Sevin) and bromophos. Or, to control millipedes, add BHC dust to the soil and deep dig. (Note that *centipedes* are not a pest.)

Onion Fly: The adult resembles a house fly, but it is the small young whitish grubs which do the damage.

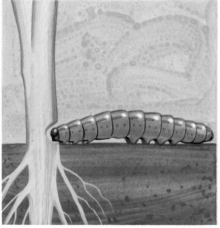

Cutworm.

Lift and destroy infected plants, making sure if possible that you capture all the grubs. Apply either calomel dust to the seed rows or diazinon granules to the soil, and calomel paste to the base of onion sets and shallots if this pest is a real problem. In fact, attack is not all that frequent, but the pest is most likely to occur in dry soil conditions.

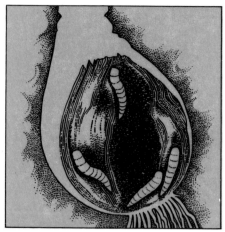

Onion Fly.

Pea Moth: This insect lays eggs in June and July and the maggots enter the developing pea pods to tunnel into the young peas. Early crops are not affected, but spray later ones with lindane once at the start of flowering and again fourteen days later to ensure control. (Spray flowering plants in the evening to reduce the chance of damaging bees.)

Red Spider Mite: Very tiny red or yellowish-red creatures which feed on the undersides of the leaves, turning them a rusty colour. Attacks from this pest are most likely in a hot, dry atmosphere and with severe infestations a fine webbing also occurs on the leaves. Spray infected plants regularly with water; in greenhouses spray with derris and malathion and use azobenzene smokes. Except in very hot, dry, weather, Red Spider is only a pest of crops such as tomato, peppers, melons, beans and aubergines, which are being grown in greenhouse conditions.

Pea Moth.

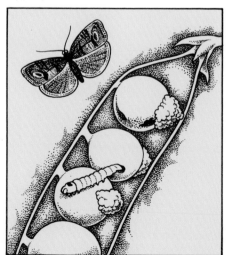

Slugs and snails: Both can be a nuisance in the garden and greenhouse, and are encouraged by damp conditions. Signs of attack, which usually occur at night, are slime trails and plants with holes chewed in their leaves and stems. Look underneath pots and boxes to find slugs in the day time. Both pests are easily controlled by using proprietary slug pellets or slug spray. Slug bait based on methiocarb will destroy slugs even in wet weather, but there is a chance that they will recover from metaldehyde-based materials in wet conditions. If there is a heavy rain fall, therefore, it

Red Spider Mite Damage.

Slugs and Snails.

may be necessary to repeat the metaldehyde bait application. You can entice and trap slugs by placing empty half grapefruit and orange skins upturned on the soil.

The small black slug which lives below ground and eats holes in potatoes and other root crops is the most difficult to control. Growing early potatoes and lifting them early is the most effective way to avoid exces-

sive damage. Improving drainage and watering the soil with liquid slug preparations will help too. Pieces of potato stuck on canes and pushed into the soil in spring make good slugtraps.

White Fly.

Whitefly: A light-coloured fast moving insect and a persistent pest of greenhouse plants. It can be controlled by spraying with resmethrin, which allows the crop to be harvested within 24 hours of spraying.

Wireworm: The distinctive golden larvae of wireworm attack root crops such as potatoes, carrots and parsnips and will also eat through many seedling roots. This pest occurs particularly in turf so watch for it after digging up grass. Break larvae you find in half to destroy them and use soil chemicals like bromophos and lindane for control. As with black slugs, a trap can be made using potatoes.

Wireworm.

DISEASES AND THEIR CONTROL

Asparagus Rust: Rusty brown powder on the foliage and black streaks on the stems in late summer. Cut the stems to the ground and burn to prevent the disease spreading. The 'Tree Onion', (rather like shallots but growing on a single stem 3 ft (90 cm) high), can also be infected with this disease.

Asparagus Violet Root Rot: Premature yellowing of the foliage and the presence of violet fungus strands on the roots. This condition is most likely to occur on old plants, but the disease will spread outwards to other plants in late summer so carefully lift and destroy those that are infected. Avoid planting root crops in infected soil; rotate with green crops, such as cabbage, which will be unaffected.

Black Leg of Potatoes: Plants turn yellow prematurely and will not develop fully. If you lift yellowing plants you will find they have a black shrivelled root and the tuber will probably be wet, slimy and have an unpleasant smell. Cold, wet soils encourage this disease which you can discourage by rotating crops and planting certified disease-free seed.

Botrytis: Commonly called 'Grey Mould' because of the fluffy grey mould which develops on the soft brown areas caused by this disease. Its brown-coloured spots may appear on the leaves of lettuce in winter and, to a lesser extent, crops such as peppers in the autumn and broad beans from December, but especially from April to July. Avoid cold, damp conditions for lettuce under glass and clear all old plant remains immediately. Control with dusts and sprays using materials such as benlate and thiram.

Blossom End Rot.

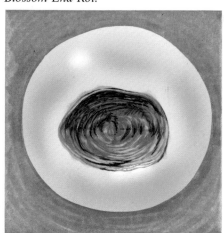

Buck-eye Rot and Blossom End Rot of Tomatoes: Buck-eye Rot causes concentric brown rings on the plant's lower trusses. It is splashed up from the soil, so be careful when watering with a hose. Blossom End Rot is much more common and is a dark green circular spot at the tip of the fruit which turns brown or black and is of a shrunken, leathery texture. It is caused by irregular watering, and it can be avoided by keeping the plants evenly moist – not subjecting them alternately to very wet and then very dry states.

Celery Leaf Spot.

Celery Leaf Spot: Brown spots on the leaves with tiny black fungus spores in the centre are symptoms of this disease. Seed is treated to avoid initial infection and, you can use bordeaux and zineb sprays subsequently to give lasting control.

Club root of Brassicas: Also called 'finger and toe' disease because of the plump round root swellings which result from this disease. The plants look sickly, are stunted and may wilt in hot weather. Don't confuse club root swellings with the swollen galls caused by turnip gall weevil; if you cut through club root swelling it is complete with a mottled appearance – the gall weevil swelling is hollow and often the maggot will be seen inside. Clubroot disease enters the root from the soil and heavy liming will control it. Add 4–5 oz per yd (100–125 gm per 0.8 sq m) immediately after clearing an infected crop. Burn all the diseased roots – if you just leave them to rot down, they can infect the soil for at least seven years. Dusting the planting hole with calomel dust and dipping the plant roots in a paste of calomel also controls the disease.

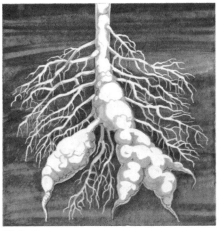

Club Root.

Damping off: Sudden death of seedlings which keel over and on close inspection have shrivelled stems at ground level. This disease infects many seeds raised indoors in pots and the use of clean compost, clean containers and clean water is fundamental to control. Fungicidal seed dressing, captan and chest-nut compounds, are a help in controlling this disease.

Foot Root of Peas and Beans: Early yellowing of the foliage, and dry shrivelling of the root and base of stem, which becomes discoloured reddish brown. Avoid replanting in infected soil and plan long rotations, i.e. three years or more between successive pea and bean crops. Applications of fungicidal seed dressing will reduce the problem.

Leaf Mould of Tomatoes, (*Cladosporium*): Yellow spots on the upper surface of the leaves and greyish mould beneath occurring from June/July onwards under glass. Warm, humid atmospheres encourage this disease and although copper sprays

Leaf Mould.

can be used to help control it, it is better to grow disease-resistant varieties.

Mildew – Powdery Mildew: Powdery white and greyish-white patches which cover the leaves and other aerial parts of the plant. Attacks are likely on such plants as cucumbers, marrows, swedes and turnips. Hot and dry conditions, especially if accompanied by heavy dew, encourage the spread of this disease and marrows and swedes grown in the garden in early autumn are likely to be subject to these conditions. Keeping plants well watered and dusting with flowers of sulphur or spraying with copper based fungicides such as bordeaux will help to keep the disease in check.

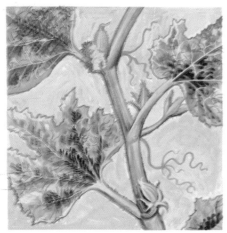

Mosiac Virus.

Downy Mildew: A greyish-brown or violet-grey growth on the undersides of leaves, with yellowish spots appearing on the upper surface. Young cabbage plants under cold glass in winter where the atmosphere is damp are vulnerable to attack and cold wet conditions will encourage attack on spinach, lettuce, peas and onions. A dry atmosphere is death to downy mildew but garden hygiene is important for control, so remove any old crop remains which would otherwise allow this disease to carry over from one year to the next.

Mosaic Virus: Virus diseases are often transmitted by greenfly, which sucks the sap from an infected plant and carries it to others. Affected plants are dwarfed, the leaves turn pale and become mottled-dark and light green. It is important to sow only clean seed, and to destroy single infected plants immediately, so the disease does not

have a chance to spread. Also control greenfly (see Aphids, page 112). Crops which are affected by mosaic virus include lettuce, marrow and tomatoes, but there are resistant varieties of

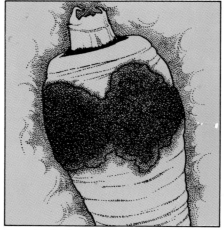

Parsnip Canker.

tomato available. It is particularly advisable to use these specially produced varieties where the disease has occurred previously.

Parsnip Canker: Rusty brown marks and cracks, especially around the top of the root. Control carrot fly (see page 112) as they will encourage the spread of this disease. Grow resistant varieties and avoid excess nitrogen in the soil by being careful with fertiliser application.

Potato blight: Brown blotches on the leaves which spread, making the lower foliage turn yellow. The disease will also spread to infect the tubers, and appears as sunken areas of reddish brown which soon spread to turn the whole tuber rotten. Damp, humid weather from July onwards encour-

Potato Blight.

ages the spread of this disease. Spray every ten to fourteen days with copper based sprays, maneb or zineb fungicides. Outdoor tomatoes can also be affected with similar damage to leaf and fruit, and may be protected in the same way.

Potato Scab: Black, rough scabby, patches on the skin of potatoes which, look unpleasant although they are peeled off before cooking. Add organic matter to the soil to help reduce the likelihood of attack. Make sure the soil contains *no* lime.

White Rot of Onions: Affects onions and also leeks, making the leaves turn yellow and die back while a white mould covers the base of the plant. This soil-borne fungus can remain in the soil for eight or more years so dig up and burn infected plants with the immediately surrounding soil. Con-

White Rot of Onion.

trol by crop rotation and dusting the seed drills with calomel. Note that the onion, 'White Lisbon', is particularly susceptible to this disease, so keep a careful watch if growing this variety.

In Conclusion

This list of pests and diseases may look formidable, but in fact it is seldom that the gardener is faced by many of them. More than half of those listed I have never personally encountered in twenty years of my home vegetable growing and none have prevented the cultivation of acceptable crops.

With judicious use of just a few chemicals – perhaps slug pellets, derris, lindane, malathion, bordeaux and calomel dust, most vegetable problems can be kept at bay and will not present a serious threat.

Weeds and their Control

Although weeds tend to grow faster and more prolifically than anything else in the garden they are really only a difficulty when they are allowed to get the upper hand. Like so many other things, the answer is to keep them constantly under control. Picking out the perennial roots of such weeds as couch grass and convolvulus, when digging, is the first essential. It may take a moment or two longer to dig over the plot as a result but removing the roots at that stage will relieve you of future problems.

Figure 115: Hoe regularly between rows of vegetables to remove annual weeds.

The vast majority of weeds – that is, all those without persistent perennial roots – can just be dug into the soil at the end of each season. You can then easily control weed growth throughout the following spring by quickly and lightly hoeing over the surface every three weeks or so. Earlier in the year, you can hoe over the plot less frequently, but as the temperature increases thus speeding up the growth of all plants – including weeds – you will find more frequent hoeing is necessary. Hoe even before you can see any weeds, as this destroys germinating weed seeds before they have time to become established.

If you find a hoe difficult to use effectively, try doing the same job with a spade, using it to chip the surface soil. Hold the blade at 45° to the surface and work backwards, chipping the soil as you go. Try to hoe at a time when it looks as if a few hours dry weather will follow: this dries out the weeds and seedling weeds as well as protecting and maintaining the desirable crumbly tilth. Remember to keep off the soil when it is wet, especially on the heavier soils. You can keep soil which has been dug, but is not sown or planted, free of weeds, by pulling a cultivator through the surface.

WEEDKILLERS

Picking out perennial roots and repeated hoeing is really all that is necessary for complete weed control, but if you feel you need some additional help there are several chemical weedkillers commercially available and many of these are quite adaptable. There are three basic types of weedkiller, the complete long term killers, the complete short term ones and the selective weedkillers. *The important thing with all of them is to follow the manufacturers' instructions exactly.*

Figure 116: Use a dribble bar for accurate placement of contact weed killers.

Long term Weedkillers

Best known of the complete long term weedkillers is *sodium chlorate*, a relatively cheap material which kills all plants for a period of months, if not years, depending on the strength of application. It has two big disadvantages; the first is its solubility which allows it to move sideways for some distance in soil moisture. Thus if you water a gravel path with dilute sodium chlorate rain water is likely to wash the chemical into adjacent grass paths and vegetable plots, where it will destroy garden plants as well as weeds. The second disadvantage is a fire risk. If, for example, dilute sodium chlorate has been used to kill grass along a fence, the dry dead grass becomes very inflammable. A dropped cigarette end

Figure 117: Although annual weeds do not present as great a problem as perennials, they should still be strictly controlled. Pictured here from l. to r. are Common Chickweed, Shepherd's Purse, Sun Spurge, Annual Meadow Grass, Annual Nettle and Groundsel.

Figure 118: Perennial weeds are often very hard to eradicate successfully. Pictured here from l. to r. they are: Dock, Couch Grass, Ground Elder, Convolvulus, Bulbous Oxalis, Horsetail.

would ignite the grass and the bottom of the fence with alarming speed. Be careful therefore if you use sodium chlorate to allow for some sideways spread from the weedkiller-watered area and to lessen the likelihood of the fire risk by applying it a few hours before a bout of heavy rain is forecast.

Slightly more expensive but with neither disadvantage are the complete long term weedkillers based on chemicals like *simazine*. They present no fire risk and as they do not easily dissolve, they remain in the surface soil after application. They are best applied to a clean, wet soil (early spring is a good time). Given this treatment all weed growth is likely to be controlled for a full season, particularly if you hoe out the odd weed which is resistant to simazine.

Figure 119: Perennial weeds may be controlled by pushing leaves into a jam jar of suitable weedkiller. This is an effective way of controlling Convolvulus

Short term weedkillers

The complete long term weedkillers really have no place on the vegetable plot but the complete short term ones can be very useful. Short term weedkillers, such as *paraquat* (usually sold under the brand name *Weedol*) destroy all green plant material they touch but as soon as they reach the soil are rendered harmless. Using a dribble bar attachment (see figure 116) on the watering can, it is possible to water between rows of vegetables to kill weeds and yet leave the vegetables unharmed. Be careful not to splash the vegetables with this material, however, because it will kill where it touches. Paraquat is very poisonous to human beings so keep the concentrate locked away and use all the dilute material once mixed (water any surplus onto spare soil where it will promptly be converted to harmless material). Never put it into harmless-looking squash bottles which may then provide a temptation to children.

One watering with paraquat will knock out the annual weeds. Repeated watering with paraquat will be necessary to wear down and eventually knock out persistent weeds with perennial roots like convolvulus, couch grass and ground elder.

Selective Weedkillers

Perennial weeds can also be killed by very careful applications of selective weedkillers. A good example is provided by the selective lawn weedkillers, which, when diluted and watered on grass, kill most broad-leaved weeds yet leave the grass unharmed. Diluted

lawn weedkillers can be painted on the leaves of bindweed (convolvulus), docks and other perennial weeds in a vegetable plot. The weed leaves will take up the weedkillers and are destroyed, while the vegetables continue to thrive. Another way to destroy weeds selectively is to pull away several stems, for example of convolvulus, and push these into a jar of diluted selective weedkiller. Spot applications in this way are useful to check perennial weeds in perennial crops.

A simple way of removing perennial weeds such as ground elder and couch grass is to cover the infested area with a deep mulch of 4 in (10 cm) or more of peat. The weed roots come up from the soil, run through the peat and may be lifted and shaken out.

Figure 120: These weeds grow commonly on poorly drained soil. They are from l. to r.: Common Sedge, Lady's Smock, Common Rush and Forget-me-not.

Storage of Vegetables

Brussels sprouts, parsnips and savoys are among the comparatively few vegetables you can gather fresh from the garden in winter. This does not mean, however, that you cannot enjoy your own home-grown produce throughout the year, for there are a number of crops which you can harvest in bulk and then use from store as you want them. In addition it is not always practical or possible to gather the growing winter crops – parsnips will very often be frozen into the ground after a severe frost, which can occur even in temperate regions, and anyone who has gathered sprouts covered with hoar frost will not be in a hurry to repeat the experience!

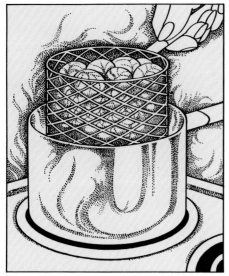

Figure 121: Most vegetables must be blanched before freezing.

FREEZING

There are various different ways of storing vegetables, and the useful life of most crops can be extended. More and more homes are now equipped with deep freezers which enable an instant supply of almost any type of vegetable throughout the year. Many vegetable varieties have been specifically bred to suit the commercial growers who are contracted to deep freeze processing factories, and these varieties are also available in seed form to home gardeners.

Nearly all special freezing varieties have been so developed that the whole crop will mature at once. Fields of peas, beans and brussels sprouts for example are grown to be ready at all the same time, so that machine harvesting or complete field clearance may be done at one go. If one of your aims in growing your own vegetables is to make sure your deep freeze is well

stocked up with garden produce to see you through the winter, you may well like to grow some of these specially produced freezing varieties. However, those people who would rather have fresh vegetables from the garden over the longest period, it is probably better to stick to growing the ordinary varieties.

The growing of vegetables can never be entirely predictable, owing to the vagaries of the weather and so on. If you do happen to get a sudden glut of peas or beans – perhaps more than the family can eat – you can freeze the surplus in polythene bags in the freezer section of an ordinary domestic fridge. Put them into the bags after you have prepared them for the table – and you will have the equivalent of a week or two longer supply of vegetables. Deep freeze owners will be familiar with the preparation of vegetables for freezing; most need to be blanched in boiling water for a minute or two, then cooled and sealed in plastic bags or plastic containers.

There are several vegetables that are suitable for freezing – the popular ones are found in the supermarket freezers and include particularly beans, broccoli spears, sprouts, peas, spinach and sweet corn. The succulent french or snap beans are the easiest green pods for freezing and are ideal for this kind of storage. Broad beans are excellent too, and best results will be obtained from the green-seeded varieties, which must be gathered while they are very young and succulent. In fact most crops are best gathered young but broad beans and garden peas really have to be picked at the earliest stage possible to give the best flavour.

Figure 122: Runner Beans may be stored in common salt.

Root vegetables such as carrot, parsnip and turnip can be diced and frozen, but they break with the 'gather very young' rule, for the more mature roots are best. Some crops such as sweet peppers can be frozen fresh without blanching first. Try freezing cubes of fresh melon too, if you have some to spare – in fact don't be afraid to experiment – most vegetables that are cooked before eating can be deep frozen. Asparagus, artichokes, aubergines, sliced cabbage, celery and courgettes, pieces of cauliflower and spinach are all good examples. Avoid only the water filled succulent salad crops like chicory, endive, lettuce, cucumbers and tomatoes (unless tomatoes are wanted for frying or stewing.) If you are unsure of the correct preparation method for freezing any specific vegetable, you should consult one of the specialist publications.

Figure 123: Stages of clamping vegetables.

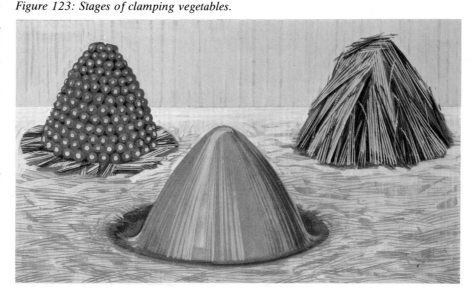

Figure 124: Dry herbs by hanging in bunches or spreading on trays. Rub between hands when dry and sieve to remove large pieces. Store in labelled jars.

SALT STORAGE

Some blanched vegetables can de stored in a brine solution, and salt is also useful to store runner beans. Wash, string and slice the beans just as for cooking. Cover the base of a large jar or plastic container with ½ in (1 cm) or so of salt and put a layer of sliced beans 1 in (2·5 cm) deep on top. Fill the jar with alternate layers of beans and salt until it is full. Leave for a day or so, during which time the beans will settle and you will have to add more layers. When the container is almost full, cover with a last layer of salt, then seal and store it. When you want to use the beans, wash them several times in fresh, cold water to remove excess salt before cooking in the normal way.

Figure 125: Hold onions by the stems and string together firmly.

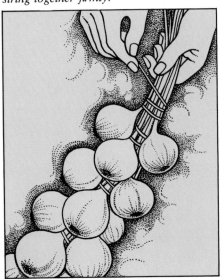

STORING IN CLAMPS AND IN PEAT AND SAND

Such methods of storage as freezing, salting, pickling and bottling are all more in the province of cooks than the gardener, and there are various ways in which vegetables can be stored in the garden. The traditional system for all winter-stored root crops whether potatoes, carrots, beetroot, celeriac or whatever, is clamping. For this you will need some straw and a patch of clear soil in the vegetable garden. Cover the soil with the straw and heap the harvested roots onto it. Surround the heap with straw and dig a ditch around the heap throwing soil from the trench over the straw. If you live in an area that is prone to heavy frost make sure you have a good layer of straw and a good deep layer of soil. If you are in a milder region, leave a small tuft of straw sticking out of the top of the clamp to allow air to escape.

Most gardens will not yield sufficient roots to fill large free-standing clamps however, and so instead make small heaps either in a shed or against a sheltered fence. Space the vegetables between layers of sand or peat and, if possible, cover with sacking and polythene to prevent the sand freezing.

The easiest way of all to store the small quantity of roots produced in most gardens each autumn, is in boxes of dry peat. Peat which feels dry to the touch, in fact contains quite a quantity of moisture, and if you use it to surround such roots as carrots, beetroot, turnip and chicory it will prevent them drying out and shrivelling. It is a good insulator and will protect the vege-

tables against quite severe frost. If it becomes frozen you can break through the outer frozen crust to get access to the roots which will remain unaffected. If, on the other hand, you store the roots in damp sand, a frost will seal them in, making it impossible to get to them until it thaws out again.

The lighter coloured, golden moss peats are better for root crop storage than the black ones in my experience. Whatever peat you use it can of course be dug into the soil or used for some other garden purpose when you have used all the stored vegetables.

The laziest, but quite effective way of storing root vegetables is to lift them, place a layer of peat in the soil, and spread out a layer of roots and so on until all the roots are covered. Protect the heap from rain by a covering of polythene held down by burying the edges under soil.

If all these methods are just too much trouble for you, you can store roots in hessian or paper bags, and keep them in a shed or any other cool place. Don't use polythene bags – they hold moisture and the condensation that collects on the inside of the bag is likely to make the roots go soft. Potatoes will store well in paper sacks as long as they are kept in a cool frost-free building.

DRYING

Warm air drying, usually with warmth from the sun, is another method of extending the useful life of vegetables and herbs. Herbs in fact require somewhat special treatment but bulb onions and shallots for example, if gathered when they are fully

Figure 126: Onions hanging in store in a net (left), strung together (right).

developed, may be ripened and dried in the sun for storage and used round to the next season's crop.

Drying and ripening can be done outside on the soil, or alternatively you can construct wire-netting-based racks as frames on which you put the onions and other crops. These are effective as they alow air movement from all sides. If crops are moved to the greenhouse or put under frames the drying will be even faster.

When they are quite dry and their skins crackly and brittle, onions can be stored by hanging in ropes or spaced out in shallow trays.

Drying herbs is an effective storage method that gives supplies of culinary flavourings the year round. Collect the foliage of parsley, thyme, sage and mint before the plants start to flower. This usually means you can take two crops – one in July and another in September.

Cut the leaves on short stems using a sharp knife or secateurs for woody plants like thyme and sage. Group them in small bunches for ease of handling or drop the short sprigs into a fine mesh sieve. You can then either hang up the bunches or spread the stems in trays to dry. The secret of successful herb drying is to subject them to rapid drying in quite hot air, up to 100°F (38°C) out of direct sunshine. Although the foliage should be cut in full sun so it is dry and thereafter left to wilt in the sun for an hour or so, don't leave it in full sun to dry completely. This would take two to three weeks, and much of the flavour would be destroyed.

When it has reached the stage of being brittle, rub the sprigs between your hands to snap down to usable size. You can sieve the rubbed herbs to take out the large and dusty particles, and then store them in sealed jars. Herbs treated in this way can be stored almost indefinitely. Remember they have a stronger flavour than their fresh counterparts.

If you want to dry peas, beans and celery seed, for example, to store leave them on the plant to do most of the ripening and drying. You must then catch the crop just as the first few seeds fall naturally. Gather the heads of celery and pods of peas and put them in shallow paper-lined trays and paper bags to completely ripen. If you gather a few days before the natural release of seed, the crop will be quite all right, and the seeds will finish ripening in the pod and husk.

STORAGE AT A GLANCE CHART

Crop	Storage Method	Period of Use from Store
ARTICHOKE (Globe)	Deep freeze	To the next crop
ARTICHOKE (Jerusalem)	Clamp or paper bag	October – May
ASPARAGUS	Deep freeze	To the next crop
AUBERGINE	Deep freeze	To the next crop
BEANS (Broad)	Deep freeze	To the next crop
BEANS (French)	Deep freeze	To the next crop
BEANS (Haricot or Butter)	Dry	The year round
BEANS (Runner)	In salt	The year round
BEETROOT	Clamp or in peat/sand	Almost to the next crop
BROCCOLI	Deep freeze	To the next crop
BRUSSELS SPROUTS	Deep freeze	To the next crop
CABBAGE (winter keeping)	In trays or on wire racks	November to March
CABBAGE – RED	Pickle in vinegar	The year round
CARROT	Clamp or in peat/sand	November to April
CAULIFLOWER	Deep freeze sprigs of flowering head	To the next crop
CELERIAC	Clamp or in peat/sand	November to March
CELERY (blanched stems)	Deep freeze	To the next crop
CHICORY	Store roots in peat/sand	Forced February to April.
COURGETTE	Deep freeze	To the next crop
MARROWS	Ripe fruits hung in string bag in frost free shed	Several weeks into the winter
MELON	Deep freeze	To the next crop
ONIONS	In ropes or trays	To the next crop
PARSNIP	Clamp or in peat/sand	November – May
PEAS	Deep freeze	To the next crop
PEAS	Dried	The year round
PEPPERS	Deep freeze	To the next crop
POTATOES	Clamp or in paper bags	To the next crop
RADISH (winter)	Clamp or in peat/sand	To the spring radish
RHUBARB	Deep freeze	To the next crop
SALSIFY	Clamp or in peat/sand	Winter and early spring
SCORZONERA	Clamp or in peat/sand	Winter and early spring
SHALLOTS	In ropes or trays	To the next crop
SPINACH	Deep freeze	To the next crop
SWEDE	Clamp or paper bags	Winter and spring
SWEETCORN	Deep freeze	To the next crop
TOMATO	Hang up unripened trusses or store in boxes	October to December
TURNIP	Clamp or in peat/sand	To the next crop

Calendar of Work - Spring

Early spring

Harvest: Brussels sprouts, kale, and cabbage as spring greens. Lift vegetables overwintering in the garden such as Jerusalem artichokes, carrots, parsnips, leeks.

Sow – indoors: Lettuce, cabbage, cauliflower, celery to plant out later.

Sow – outdoors: Broad beans, round-seeded peas, radish and round-seeded spinach either when conditions allow, or under cloches.

Plant: Jerusalem artichokes and shallots, when soil conditions allow.

Cultivate: Seed potatoes by putting in shallow trays in a light frost-free place to develop short shoots.
Apply general fertiliser to plot and cultivate it into the surface when preparing a fine crumbly surface in readiness for seed sowing.

Protect: Young seedlings and pea and bean seeds from slugs and mice attack by putting down bait.

Mid-Spring

Harvest: New green shoots from brussels sprouts as green vegetable, turnip tops and spring cabbage as greens. Lift any remaining leeks and heel them in for use in the next few weeks. It is also advisable to lift any remaining root vegetables now. Store them in the recommended way if necessary.

Sow – indoors: Celery (self-blanching and trench varieties) and brussels sprouts for early crops.

Sow – outdoors: *Broad beans, brussels sprouts, *cabbage, carrot, *lettuce, leeks, onions, parsley, parsnips, *peas, *radish, *spinach, turnips.

Plant: Onion sets, broad beans and peas from the earlier indoor sowing.

Cultivate: Apply nitrogen fertiliser top dressing to spring cabbage and overwintered lettuce crops. Pull earth up over asparagus crowns so they are well covered, to provide blanched stems. Start routine hoeing to control weeds as surface soil dries.

Protect: As many of the outdoor-sown crops as possible with cloches to give early crops and better germination. Polythene tunnel cloches also prevent sparrows eating lettuce and other emerging seedlings.

Late Spring

Harvest: Start cutting asparagus, sprouting broccoli, kale, spring cabbages, and pulling radish. Clear brussels sprouts and winter cabbage. Leave the woody stems in the air to dry out, before burning them.

Sow – indoors: (Towards the end of the period) aubergines, peppers, tomatoes, runner beans and sweet corn.

Sow – outdoors: beetroot, *cabbage, *carrots, cauliflowers, onions (for pickling), *salad onions, turnips.

Plant: Early potatoes, globe artichoke sets and cauliflowers from the earlier indoor sowing.

Cultivate: Soil and dig trench for celery. Start to erect stick or net support for early peas. Continue regular hoeing to control weeds.

Protect: Early crops from cold winds, (twiggy sticks around peas will be a help).

* Successional sowings

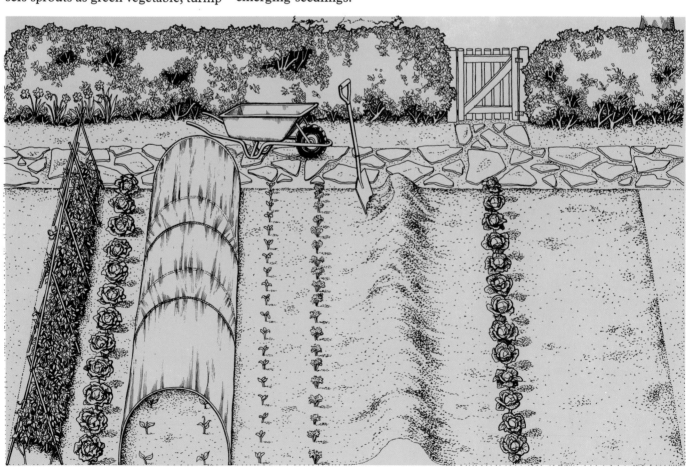

Summer

Early Summer
Harvest: Asparagus, spinach, spring cabbage, sprouting broccoli, lettuce, radish, salad onions.

Sow – indoors: (Early in the period) aubergines, cucumbers, marrows, melons, peppers and tomatoes.

Sow – outdoors: Beans – french and runner, winter greens – kale, savoys and sprouting broccoli and cabbage, *carrots, *lettuce, *beetroot, swede and sweet corn. At the end of the period sow ridge cucumbers and marrows.

Plant: Indoor-raised beans and sweet corn under cloches and celery outside. Plant brussels sprouts and other winter green crops as soon as they are large enough.

Cultivate: Pull soil up and around potatoes, covering the emerging young shoots if frost is imminent. Maintain regular hoeing and in drier areas apply a 2–3 in (5–8 cm) mulch of peat and well-rotted compost to retain moisture in the soil.

Protect: Tender crops with cloches or with newspaper at night if frost is forecast. Keep a watch out for greenfly and use a protective spray at the first signs of attack.

Midsummer
Harvest: Finish cutting asparagus and start picking broad beans, cauliflowers and peas. Continue gathering cabbage, lettuce, spring onions, radish and spinach.

Sow – outdoors: Swedes, *beetroot *carrots, *lettuce, *peas, turnips, french and runner beans.

Plant: All tender vegetables such as aubergines, cucumbers, peppers, tomatoes and marrows outside. A few late potatoes can also be planted. Continue planting out leeks and winter green vegetables.

Cultivate: Support crops like runner beans and tomatoes by erecting stakes and strings. Continue thinning out seedlings to the required spacing and hoeing to eliminate weeds.

Protect: Broad beans from black fly attack by pinching out the growing tips of plants infested with this pest. Place nets over peas if birds are eating the peas in the pods.

Late Summer
Harvest: Most crops – e.g. dwarf beans, cabbage, cauliflower, globe artichokes, peas, carrots, turnips, lettuce and early potatoes and shallots.

Sow – outdoors: Spring cabbage, at the end of the period, also *carrots, *lettuce, *parsley, *radish and turnip.

Plant: Complete winter green transplanting.

Cultivate: Apply liquid fertiliser to beans, celery and tomatoes, every ten to fourteen days for the biggest crops. Water occasionally, (or well in hot, dry weather).

Protect: Potatoes in warm damp weather against blight by spraying with a copper fungicide. Give some shade to emerging seedlings and crops like melons in very hot sunshine, by using cloches that have been painted white.

Autumn

Early Autumn

Harvest: Most crops – including a start on sweet corn, tomatoes, marrows and ridge cucumbers. Lift shallots and dry out in the sun before storing for winter use.

Sow – outdoors: Winter spinach, spring cabbage (early in the period), onions for overwinter, spring salad onions.

Cultivate: Continue hoeing to control weeds, watering and liquid feeding where necessary. Keep side-shooting tomatoes and training cucumbers where they are cordon-grown.

Protect: Ripening onions and shallots from heavy rainfall to prevent re-growth and split bulbs. Harvest crops as soon as they are ready to prevent rapid ageing in hot conditions.

Mid-Autumn

Harvest: Beans – french and runners, beetroot, cabbage, carrots, cauliflowers, cucumbers, lettuce, marrow and turnips. It is a good time to lift potatoes (leave them to dry for an hour or two before storing for winter use). Make sure you have stored crops such as onions before the end of this period.

Sow: Lettuce, onions to overwinter and turnips for turnip tops.

Plant: Spring cabbage from the late summer sowing.

Cultivate: Soil as potatoes are lifted to prepare for cabbage and other crops. This is a good time to start another compost heap as the autumn clean-up is under way.

Protect: A good time to erect polythene-covered structures, both cloches and greenhouses. They will then survive two winters and at least one full summer.

Late Autumn

Harvest: The first brussels sprouts and the last of all crops likely to be destroyed by frost. Lift and store all the root crops as they mature. Complete lifting potatoes and put in store for use through the winter.

Sow – outdoors: Lettuce and round-seeded peas and broad beans (towards the end of this period) to overwinter, ideally under cloches.

Plant: Spring cabbage before soil conditions get very wet and cold.

Cultivate: Start autumn digging and cut down the old stems on asparagus. This is a good time to dig in well-decayed garden compost.

Protect: Endive to give blanched hearts and start to force chicory in pots indoors.

Winter

Early Winter
Harvest: Brussels sprouts, winter spinach beet, cabbage and the last of the cauliflowers. Start lifting trench grown celery (it will have more flavour after frost). Complete lifting root vegetables to store overwinter.

Sow: Round-seeded peas and broad beans, ideally under cloches.

Cultivate: Complete the big clear-up by storing canes and stakes, composting old leaves and plant remains and burning old stems of crops like runner beans and peas. Dig any vacant soil.

Mid-Winter
Harvest: Check stored vegetables occasionally and remove any that show signs of rotting. Continue to gather brussels sprouts, spinach beet and winter cabbage.

Sow – indoors: Onions at the end of the period, (but only if you want really big onions next year).

Cultivate: Continue digging if not completed.

Protect: Tender plants like globe artichoke by putting some old pea stems around the base and pulling soil up around them. Protect tender stored vegetables like potatoes from the frost.

Late Winter
Harvest: Winter-rooted green vegetables and then use other vegetables from store. Continue to force chicory for winter salads.

Sow – indoors: Mustard and cress for winter salads.

Plan: For the coming year. Select the varieties you wish to grow and secure supplies.

Cultivate: This is a good time to apply lime to dug soil which tends to be acid. Cut sticks for peas and bean support.

Index

Acknowledgements

We are indebted to the following organisations and individuals for permission to reproduce photographs:
Floraprint Limited
Glasshouse Crops Research Institute
Murphy Chemical Limited
Richard Sharpe Studios
Sutton Seeds Limited
Syndication International
Thompson & Morgan (Ipswich) Limited
Michael Warren